Black MADONNAS

ORIGIN

Karyn Crisis

*This book is dedicated to
Davide Tiso, Ernie, Cybele*

Special thanks to Carlo Napolitano

CHAPTERS AND SUBCHAPTERS

CHAPTER 1: STONE

Black MADONNAS ORIGIN
Black Magnetic Stone Mountain

The origin of Black Madonnas takes us to the center of pre-christian worldwide beliefs about the Cosmos and:
- its Highest Holy central place
- its structure, realms and landscapes, its waters, passageways and portals,
- its Divinities who've been placed under specific categorizations (by Duty to Divine Motion and realms of access) and who've been identified by root words whose etymology proves to be the same worldwide
- its Protectors,
- its Highest Divine Force: Motion and aspects of its mechanization, venerated by Divinities and humans alike,
- and its Creation.

Which leads us to the parallels existing in this earthly realm:
- the mapped heavens on earth
- the Creation process of earthly cities and land masses (the island cities of myths)
- the Creation of humans
- celestial-to-earth alignment of altars, temples and other structures for the purpose of connecting with Deities and being *right* with the Cosmos, *right* here meaning an indication of Motion turning in the proper direction,
- the veneration of Deities believed to embody specific natural items that relate to their Cosmic function, which then become natural conduits to consciousness of said Deities or cosmic zones of access as well as being descriptors of duty to Divine Motion.

Viewing **Black Madonnas** through perspectives of the peoples who envisioned the Universe in a specifically detailed way, expressing through oral methods of sophisticated organization their belief systems + spiritual system of symbols and who created record keeping systems to perpetuate them, inevitably unlocks other mysterious symbols due to their interconnectivity. It also unlocks the powers and presence of the **Black Madonnas**.

Within this book can be found the Origin of **Black Madonnas**, categorizations of some other specific Deities for the purpose of shining a broader light upon the role of **Black Madonnas** in the Cosmos, and several additional symbols whose origins have been connected to **Madonnas** in general, yet have been in use far longer in oral cultures before arrival of the **Madonnas** and the **Black Madonnas**. Other Deities' roles in detail and other landscapes of the Cosmos will be revealed in my next books.

The symbols shared here are worldwide archaic beliefs. While they come from Oral cultures, that is, cultures who didn't use writing to keep information gathered for use and for reference and for passing along, it's important to acknowledge that 99% of human history was never written down.[1] Generally, the people in power kept records about their power, neglecting other viewpoints. And while not spoken about due to historical burials of preceding beliefs, spiritual overthrows, censorship and more, these oral beliefs are metaphysical and can be located as the foundation of spiritual practices and religions still touted in our contemporary times.

For example, an idea I've always tried to impress during the workshops and lectures I've given on rural Italian oral traditions over the past years has been about the belief that physical matter has an energetic counterpart, and vice versa, and that each affects the other. So, found within the orally inherited medico-magical* cures for ailments such as *vermi* and *verruche* and even behind the *amaro* digestive drinks is a belief that the soul affects the physical body, and the physical body affect the soul...whether the soul of an ill person that is affecting the physical body negatively and causing illness, or the soul of a ghost or even a succubus, both the physical and energetic are entwined.

*see my books "Italian Magic : Secret Lives of Women" and "Italy's Witches and Medicine Women Vol 1" for detailed information about rural medico-Magic in Italy.

That even plants have their spirit counterparts is something found in the rural invocations of Santa Lucia for healing eyesight in small valleys of Umbria, where the *spirit* of fennel is invoked to come 'round the houses and create a circle of white light protection as well as the *spirit* of Santa Lucia, as documented by Mario Polia.*see prayer in Notes section

This belief is not unique to Italy but is also found around the world among the beliefs connected to **Black Madonnas** and their Cosmic Origin:

-*In China, The substance of all things has its image in the heavens, and its form on earth.*
-*In the Zoroastrian faith celestial things had their terrestrial counterparts.*
-*The Chaldeans who perfected the* **genethliac** *art by attaching terrestrial things to things on high, and the heavens to the lower world.* [2]

It was believed that Creation began in the Cosmos, including: the creation of conscious beings, waters, land, animals, plants and the "sun's sun" original sun and then these things were created into an earth by many Deities, including the creation of humans.

This, among other reasons, compelled people to
Mark the Heavens Upon the Earth.

"In the mid-early 1900s the last Lakota Medicine Man disclosed to an anthropologist a Lakota tradition, because he was old and about to die and he didn't know of any other Lakota who knew about it. What he shared is part of our ancient culture, that:When the Lakota did the migrations they created a winter camp and stayed there. The in the spring they broke camp..and everyone assumed they followed the herds, the berries that were growing (followed the food chain) as the Lakota tribes traveled through what is now central north America, North and South Dakota. That's not what they were doing. Their winter camp was predicated on a constellation in the sky. And when the sun entered that constellation it represented the Winter Season, and they would travel to a specific place on earth that represented their Winter Constellation. So they arrive at the Winter camp which is an earthly representation of a heavenly constellation. And that's where they spend the winter. Then when the sun enters their Spring constellation, they break camp and they go to a different camp which represents the Spring constellation. And when the Sun enters the Summer constellation....they break camp and enter a different camp that represents their summer constellation. In other words, their migration[...] is following following a Sacred Cosmology: it's following the sun through the sacred Lakota constellations.
In every camp they had a series of myths and rituals that were told, and those myths and

rituals filled with astronomical motifs. Furthermore all those camps are representations of stars in the sky, which means all the stars in the sky are representations of camps on the ground. The sky is a land map and the ground is a sky map. They have mapped them onto each others so that any Lakota who knows that can look at the sky: there's your geography map, and can look to the ground, there's your planetarium. [3]

This is a very sophisticated thing that oral cultures do, going back thousands of years.[4] So in Italy, when people claim churches to Madonnas have been arranged on mountain peaks to resemble constellations, it should not be surprising and was likely a practice that was widespread and utilized globally. And, not only did buildings represent constellations, but items of veneration did as well.

EARTH: IMITATION OF CELESTIAL SPACE

"Cosmicizing the land"[5] is the way oral peoples marked Heavens Upon the Earth; their observed as well as spiritually experienced knowledge of: Divinities, celestial structures, star movements and their affects upon earth, beliefs about water and metals, potent natural objects such as trees and stones that were animated by Divinity, and use of color. Adding to this list: wells, stone pillars, wood poles, round towers, omphalos stones, *ziggurats*, and *dobongs* to name a few common ones.

Marking the Heavens Upon the Earth is also a process of remembrance, which sets and leaves pointers towards the heavens, using naturally existing or synthetically created symbols derived from the Cosmos itself and its meanings, thus Marking Divinity Upon the earth is connected and inseparable to these oral beliefs.

A very brief list of these earthly parallels set to emulate Cosmic cycles and structures and various areas (of knowledge, of healing, for examples) or for communication with Deities are:

- **Auguring the 4 Cardinal points** and using these directions to: set not only foundations of temples but also their entry and exit doors, to organize burial sites, and such was done at this Great Stone Buddhist Stupa at Takht-e-Rostam in Afghanistan believed to be built in the 5th or 4th century AD, and the Great Stupa at Sanchi located on a hilltop at Sanchi Town in Raisen District of the State of Madhya Pradesh, India.
- **Using natural items** to connect with the Deities they represent both in celestial space and on terrestrial earth: items that have fallen to earth like meteorites or others that represent Deity's ability to traverse the cosmic realms according to what access they have, and to communicate to the Spirit of specific Deities they belong to such as was done with trees and stones in their natural forms long before they were carved into human imagery and implanted onto celestial divinity.
- **Setting the navel** , or center, of a city with an Omphalos stone, which represents a marker made by a Divinity (using the stone spear of Polar Deities with a Fleur-de-Lis on it apex), an instruction to begin a city on this spot, such as was indicated by the Japanese Creator Deities Izanagi and Izanami, which would then become the "center of the world" which might have been instructed by a star, for example. While these generation stories are of myth, on earth the oracles would sit on these omphalos stones, thus speaking for and mimicking Polestar Deities who sit on their stone thrones in the Center of the Cosmos.
- The **building of and use of Ziggurats** in 7 levels to indicate the 7 realms and for the practice of ascending those realms while on earth, and where **Black stones** were used to represent the 7 Polar Deities of the Ursa constellations such as at Uruk.

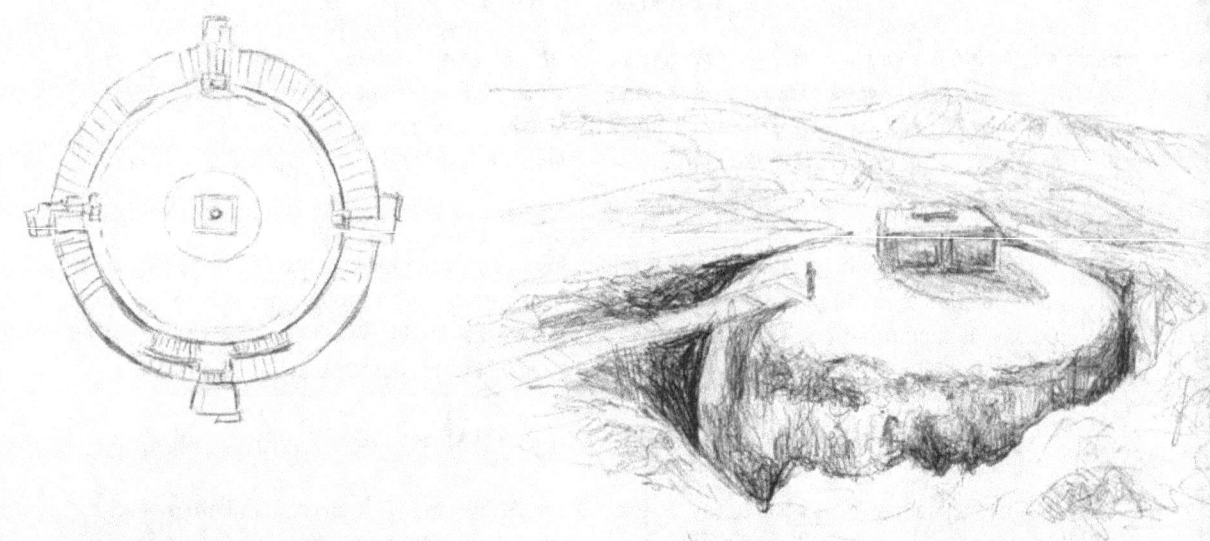

The stupa itself is a representation of Heaven's Stone Mountain and the Heavens Palace, celestially situated at the highest point in cosmos: the Celestial Polar North, and on top of the Universe, the axis from which 4 cardinal directions emanate…built as a replica on earth. In the diagram the Pillar Axis is in the center, we see 4 Gates of Heaven one must gain entry to for the Palace and its Arcana. Placed on top of an earthly mountain it represents a parallel of this Highest of the High places. Archaic temples built from these beliefs are often structured in a round shape, representing the dance of the celestial stars around the Mountain round which entire Universe revolves..while many other earthly temples representing Deity quarters /stone houses of Deities are square, square representing the earth plane in general. This is the Mountain in which **Black Madonnas** dwell.

- **The digging of wells** to commemorate the Sacred Waters that are located originally in celestial space near the Black Stone Mountain of **Black Madonnas**.
- Piles of **stones, branches, and rags** assembled to emulate the Black-Stone Heavens-Mountain, its Universe-Tree-Axis and the Polar Deities of this Highest of High cosmic zone. A pile of stones was made in a mountain shape, which holds up a tree post which then has rags of fabric tied to the top. In Tibet these are called *dobongs*, and the Korean Buddhist version is called *obos*.
- Use of **pillars, columns, obelisks, tree poles, round towers, and cone**/conical/dome-shaped hats in or around temples as well as in veneration of specific Deities to represent aspects of the Universe-Tree-Axis that connects to the Black Stone Mountain.
- Christmas **Trees** and Christmas **Boxes** and **Baskets** (see my next book for expansion on this)
- Repetitive **numerical use** of universally important Constellations and Asterisms due to their proximity to the celestial area of: Black Stone Mountain, the 4 Cardinal points and 8 half-cardinal points (even 16); and usage of numbers that represent Original Creator Deity Triads (the pre-christian trinity) and the zodiacal 12, along with the 7 of both Ursa Major and Ursa Minor.
- The global use of **specific colors** to indicate a connection to a specific area of the Cosmos (and later, to dress human-image-designed representations of Deity in these colors) to indicate Categorization of such Deity, alluding to: realm, duty to Divine Motion of the Universe, type of sacrifices made, relationship to Humans, and as indicators of a Deity's ability to travel the cosmos.

In other words, re-creating celestial structures
on the material earthly world
using items and directional signals of Cosmic origin
which exist, in parallel, on earth.

CHAPTER 1: STONE

The mediums created by oral peoples to record knowledge gained from Deity as well as through direct observation of the Cosmic movements and their affects on earth were used to: Remember, Organize and Communicate all without the use of the written word. In fact, the teachings of Mystery Schools and insider spiritual knowledge were never written down at all, that is, without punishment or even death, so that we will never know the total truth of Origins of symbolic language.

The time I've spend learning rural traditions in Italy made it clear to me that these orally inherited rituals and traditions were very old, as I was told by Italian elders, and I also began to see signs of these types of traditions in other cultures anywhere I looked. I was so excited to hear, this past year, interviews with Dr John Knight Lundwall on YouTube via the MythVision channel because he describes, from a scholarly and far-reaching researched historical view-point, exactly what I was experiencing in the countrysides of many Italian regions. At the same time, he acknowledges all the shortcomings of scholarly work.

PERFORMING MEMORIES OF CELESTIAL KNOWLEDGE

I offer here a very brief list of **Bringing Heavenly Happenings into Perpetual Memory and down to earth,** such as: star disappearances and reappearances i.e. Resurrection, Creation stories, and other Mythic Templates, along with a very brief list of **Connecting Humans to the Higher Consciousness of Deity** and/or expressing teachings of Deity:

Somatic rituals
Myths
Rhymes and prayers
Veneration of Deity

These are oral methods of gathering information and communicating it to others, whether just to a single inheritor of medico-magical healing cures in rural Italy from an elder to a healer-to-be, or for whole communities who celebrate seasonal ritual traditions, all done without the use of writing, and so effectively remembered that they are still performed, even if layers of knowledge and understanding have been lost: the structure remains.

This is all relevant to the Origin of **Black Madonnas** and for the symbolism embedded in their images, myths, pilgrimages and processions. **A deeper look:**

SOMATIC RITUAL

Somatic Rituals: the use of dances, songs, processions, and rural healing magic are the performance of Memories among groups of people combined with actions, sounds, and natural items, encoded with Celestial knowledge. Processions of Black Madonna icons are examples of Somatic Rituals.

For oral peoples rituals are almost exclusively performed in community by those who are initiated into the inner secrets. This is a mark of oral cultures: group work, just as the stars in celestial space are moving along with the celestial "waters" and other elements. In the case of Italy, for example, communities still enact these rituals even if the original meanings have been lost.

Somatic Rituals are also performed on specific dates of specific months, because they are telling a celestial story about a particular movement that occurs in the sky at the same time it's being performed in parallel on earth: *the story keeps celestial time.*The structure of these rituals is multifunctional and centers on the idea of performing cosmic knowledge so as to remember the components of a celestial event such as:

- which celestial Motion is being performed. **Black Madonnas** are a personification of the most important Motion in the Cosmos as you'll learn here.

- veneration of the particular Deity or Deities, as monotheism came into play only with the literate outing of christianity and the printing press. Deities are associated with specific months or solstice dates, for example.

- for propitiation : to bring the rains to areas in drought for example, or to request abundance and healing. For example, a Cypriot Greek somatic ritual was to take a statue of the Virgin Mary through the streets in hopes of bringing rain. [6]

- to teach actual knowledge encoded in singing and dancing…the amount of steps, any costumes worn, words hiding meanings in plain site, and performances mimicking movement of celestial bodies of note.

Somatic rituals handed-down and inherited in ritual and used solo are like the ones I've written about in "Italian Magic: Secret Lives of Women" and "Italy's Witches and Medicine Women". These medico-magical rituals of rural Italy are from the oral tradition of Guaritrici (healers) who inherit cures for various soul and/or physical ailments *on specific times of the year* that are wholly memorized and use: channeled energy, encoded prayers/rhymes, *segnature* or markings made by hands on the body of a patient, local ingredients such as: water, oil, reeds, vines, animal parts…and a specific routine combining these into a medico-magical formula that have a sympathy towards the condition. While there are herbalists curing with internally taken herbs and steam baths and fumigations *suffumigi*, in the medico-magical category herbs are used symbolically and are not taken internally nor topically as a medicine. The medico-magical rituals for curing ailments often use prayers encoded with numerology, zodiacal knowledge, 4 cardinal points disguised as an equilateral cross.

Examples of Somatic Ritual in general:
- Circular dances used by Pythagoras, Jesus, Corybantes, Umbria's broom dances
- Collecting and erecting of may poles and ship masts, Processions of Madonna statues through the streets
- Pilgrimages to caves, mountain tops, water sources or repositories like wells and fountains depending on the goal of the pilgrimage and the categorization of the Deity connected with it
- Agricultural rites: harvesting, threshing, beating of wheat, winter, death.

Examples of Somatic Ritual in Italy:
- Baiardo's *Ra Barca*
- Sicily's *Ntinna a mari*
- Madonna icon processions
- Procession, *juta dei femminielli* to Montevergine
- Calabria's *Varia di Palmi*

CHAPTER 1: STONE

MYTH AS MEDIUM

Myth Making, Story telling for oral peoples are almost exclusively performed in in community by those who are initiated into the inner secrets.[7] This is a mark of oral cultures: group work, just as the stars in celestial space are moving along with the celestial waters and other elements, each performing different duties and yet working together as a whole. In rural Italy, with Processions of Madonna icons and other Somatic Rituals, family members often inherit roles and duties.

Myths are not historical fact but rather cosmic fact, [8] and therefore mythic templates create symbolic stories as a way of recording celestial knowledge and also as a way of retelling this knowledge in a way that's easy to remember because there's no writing involved.

Myths represent celestial movements of stars, planets, references to hemispheres of the Milky Way, occurrences of expanding matter, cyclic passages, creation and destruction of matter, seasonal changes that affect plant growth as well as animal migrations…all things that affect life on earth and the souls within bodies, as well as information of a calendrical nature specific to months, days, times of day and night, years…Mythic Templates offer a way to categorize layers of knowledge.

Therefore Myths use simple stories with exaggerations, enhancing memorable moments, making their memorization easy. For peoples using oral mediums, myths needed not encapsulate Historical truth to memory through story, but rather they focus on the Bigger Picture story, that of Celestial space and Divine Motion and a soul's possibilities of ascension through space, through using daily life, recognizable interpersonal dynamics (married couples with children, for example, neighbors in dispute, ill person seeking a miracle, the local farmer, specific plants and animals, arguments, wars) along with often implanted historically period-relevant and memorable Figures (kings, queens, and named warriors, for example) and even mutilations like dismemberment which are telling a Celestial event story, into Templates whose structure contained Double-Meanings (or more) and layers of Encoded knowledge in-plain-sight.

Mythic templates are found around the world, meaning that we find the same themes using local names and landscapes (a beanstalk in one area is the same as a river reed in another) with different figures plugged in: often the figures put into these stories are in fact historical (a king of the day) or instead personified celestial beings, all containing layers and layers of encoded information that play themselves out in the myth in parallels of relatable scripts: marriage, childbirth, destruction, rape, theft of divine knowledge, being consumed by the earth, triumph one over death and earning immortality through soul evolution and resurrection from a journey "on the waters". In fact, there's a **Madonna of the Snow** who exists in Italy as well as in Japan.

Examples you'll find here:
- myths of trees and earth swallowing up someone
- myths of walking on the waters/crossing the waters
- myths of the separation of heavens and earth
- myths of the Virgin Birth
- myths of the stability of the Celestial North Pole
- myths of dismemberment and mutilation

WORDS WITH DOUBLE MEANINGS

Rhymes and prayers are encoded with double meanings such as *filastrocche* which are Italian nursery rhymes which have similarities to Sumerian puns, where one word has several meanings, and known only to initiates. Rural Italian prayers to rid the evil eye and for healing other ailments are also encoded.

Why does it even matter? Because myths, local legends, "folk" tales all speak in this oral language that is symbolic. Often, when sharing these stories or prayers or rhymes I hear people say "that doesn't make sense". It's true it might not make sense to us, especially since we, as literate people reference things written down i.e. other books, other writings…forgetting that most of history's people didn't write things down, and had to use other methods of record-keeping for a great amount of information that was sometimes for everyone's usage and sometimes for the use of initiates only. *See Notes page

VENERATION OF Deities

Veneration of Deity through natural objects believed to have their origin in Celestial space, using natural items (and not always carving them into human form) that indicate Categorization of areas of the Cosmos and references to its mechanical structure, the Deities who speak through them and who dwell in these specific areas related to them, such as:
- Black stones: meteorites, aerolites, natural magnets
- trees and tree poles
- caves (natural and man-made)
- symbols such as the fleur-de-lis, rose, pansy
- mountains
- rivers
- crowns in general and The crown of 12 stars
- swaddled stones
- wells
- vines

Later developments being: Pillars, Obelisks, Columns, Wooden Figures and painted wood

CHAPTER 1: STONE

USE OF COLORS IN MARKING THE HEAVENS ON EARTH

Photo by Karyn Crisis, Napoli

Here is a brief sampling of Colors as related to **Black Madonnas**, used in the universally expressed traditions of Marking the Heavens on the Earth. These colors were used worldwide as symbols representing Cosmic zones and alluding to the Function of Cosmic Motion therein.

Black: Color of the Highest Holy place in the cosmos; The Central High Magnetic Heavens
This is the place of:
The Celestial North Pole
The Magnetic Pole and
The Polestar
the Black Stone Mountain and
the emanation of the Cardinal points from under it
The Central Black Stone Magnet
The Source of Magic
The locale of the 12 Universal Judges wearing Black caps
Dwelling of the Supreme Stone Deities including Polar Deities
The Stone Thrones of the Polar Divinities

The sanctity of Black in this region of the Cosmos is due to the belief in a central, fixed, stationary Black Magnet upon which the Universe-Tree-Axis and the entire Universe moves round. This Divine Motion of Stillness round which everything else moves is venerated as the Highest Cosmic Force.

Examples:
- The Black Magnetic Universe-Mountain stone, on which the Black stone mountain myths are based
- The Source of the Heavens-River aka The Milky Way, Source of the Moisture Element of life, Source of all Terrestrial waters.
- Home of the Heaven's Palace and its Vault and all the Divine secrets it contains
- The Source of Black Stones that Divinities throw down to earth to create "island cities" and land masses as described in myths and folk tales
- The Magnetic center from which all Black magnetic meteorites and aerolites, *heavens-fallen stones*, are venerated as retaining some of the spirit of Deities in this zone
- The Celestial polar zone that Black natural magnet stones point to, which is why they are used in compasses

All Black magnetic meteorites comprised of as much as 90% iron fall to earth from here, it is believed, which is why they have the name *heavens-fallen stones*. [9] Their earthly parallels, natural magnets, are comprised of **iron oxide** and used universally for the compass, originally constructed as magnetic stones floating on terrestrial WATER which is celestially what the Black Magnet source does in celestial waters, point to this celestial Polar zone.

Painting by Karyn Crisis

BLUE: Color of the Heavens, Color of the Cosmic waters aka celestial space of the Heavens.

Here *heavens* is defined as the celestial Universe-Ocean, the cosmic waters among which the stars are *shining like bees*. However, the Heavens-River aka Milky Way is depicted through the colors of Yellow and/or White around the world though it is believed to be the Source of all waters: both celestial and terrestrial.

The Heavens here is the astral space only allowed to traveling souls in Heavens-boats, such as the Good Ship **Ar**go, the Egyptian Boats/barques/barks, Irish celestial boats, those of India's Vedas and

Babylonian boatman of Xisuthrus, the Phoenicians, Italys *Caronte* boat and the Greek *Charon*, the boat myths in the Arabic Treatise on Stones[10] , as well as the constellation Canopus. These boats do not move across terrestrial waters but astral waters.

Painting of Our Lady of Walcourt
by Karyn Crisis

WHITE: Color of the Bright Heavens

The Bright Heavens here is defined by oral beliefs as being the Lights of the Milky Way (though in China it is referred to as the Yellow River). While the sun, moon and stars are part of the Milky Way, their Light is not part of this white color and beliefs about both the Sun, the Moon and their arrivals into veneration vary widely around the world, while beliefs about the Milky Way are universally consistent.

White here refers to, and is often interchangeable with, Silver (silver, white, yellow/gold). The Milky Way is also a representation of the Masculine and Feminine Creator Divinities separated into a Northern Hemisphere and a Southern Hemisphere, explained in myths which depict the Separation of Heavens and Earth.

Some examples of White being used to describe celestial places:
- The White Wall of the Egyptians
- Divinities of the Egyptian 8 Stars, the *august who were before the gods, the Great of the first time* represented by 4 white-heavens boats and 4 Black heavens-boats which refer to zodiacal powers. [11]
- **Agni**, the great holy white god of the Vedas
- Whiteness as Brightness, Color of the Universe-Tree and Tree of Life, of the: Cabiric gods, Tree of the golden apples of Immortality; Yggdrasill ash, Avestan haoma; Irmensauele "the universe-column sustaining all things" of German antiquity, etc. [12]
  - the Whiteness of the soma and houma and graha (holy drinks of the gods which impart sacred secret knowledge)

- *Whiteland* in the Norse myth of 3 princesses in the heavens (which refer to a Triad Divinity)
- Aztlan, which means Whiteness of the Heavens, locale of the Mexican 7-caved Divine Universe-Mountain also called Teo-Culhuacan mountain of the gods.
- Whitefoot, the Heavens-Walker of the Day, as opposed to the Heavens-Walker of the Night of the Irish Feni Triad
- Shrine throne of the Mighty Mother Zikum of the Akkadian mystical tree, which was a dark pine with a crystal White crown that spread towards to heavens-vault [13]
- Color of the Heavens-Vault and color of the egg of Chaos
- White Gold, the name for silver as used in Sanskrit and by the Egyptians whose root is **Arg** like in **Ar**gos, meaning *shining, myriad-eyed heavens*
- The White Thorn growing on the heavens-mountain Pelion which had the power to make the body insensible to winter's cold.

There is a fascinating worldwide usage in myth of the cosmic use of both Black and White being interchangeable and which represent the Universe ordering itself (or its Deities making the order) in balance, representing Night, which was believed to come first, exchanging prevalence with the Day. This appears in myths where:
- White flags are exchanged with Black flags in equal number
- Where Deities wear White coats and Black coats and exchange them
- Black lambs jumping a fence while White lambs jump the same fence, so that each side's crossing loses no numbers

RED: Color of Sacrifices made to specific Deities, primarily the Highest Creator Deities who have Immortalized and reside in the Celestial Polar Center of the Black Magnetic Rock and Polar Deities which are located here as well.

Red also symbolizes the achievement of Immortality, which then brings us back to Sacrifices, because Deities who reach Immortality have sacrifices made to them: Blood sacrifices from humans and animals, over time simulacrum sacrifices of straw men (Italy), dolls made with dried milk (India), and more rarely cakes. Cake sacrifices were generally made to lesser Deities of other cosmic zones.

Sacrifices
Human sacrifices were given to Highest of High Deities, particularly the Polar Deities. Over time, simulacrum sacrifices (symbolic substitutes) were used in place of human flesh and blood and in place of animal flesh and blood. What became of those original human sacrifices are, in a short list:

- **straw people/dolls**: the significance of straw you'll find in this book related to the Universe-Axis-Tree. This also applies to river reeds, rushes and vines.

For example, in an ancient Roman neighborhood called the **Ar**gei (whose name will make sense as you read about its etymology in the next pages), dolls resembling humans were made out of river rushes (rushes and reeds are also used in medico-magical healing) and called **Ar**gei as well. *These were sacrifices by drowning*, and thrown from a wooden structure made of poles (a pile similar to *dobongs* or from a wooden post bridge, another connection to the Universe-Axis-Tree) into a river. **Ar**gei refers to the Deities being sacrificed to, those who dwell in **Ar**gos, the shining heavens (generally) and to the Polestar and Black Mountain (specifically).

Painting of Black Madonna/Red Madonna of London by Karyn Crisis

- **clothing and clothed dolls** as drowning sacrifices: of Japan

- **dried milk people/dolls**: the significance of milk comes from the Celestial Mountain as source of all fluids that make their way down to earth (milk, water, blood)

- **woolen people dolls:** to replace human sacrifices of children, these dolls were places at crossroads, specifically as related to Celestial Crossroads emanating from the Black Stone Mountain which you'll read about repeatedly in the coming chapters.

- **basket sacrifices:** of animals were preceded by burned human sacrifices in wicker cages at the summer solstice by the Gauls [14]

- **people dolls made of wood and straw** : buried as sacrifices in China

- living slaves buried with deceased chiefs in Fiji [15]

- **mutilated dolls** sacrifices called *enemy-sacrifice*: stabbed and hacked to pieces secretly at midnight in the Eastern districts of Bengal [16]

- **whipping**: as a replacement for child sacrifices, as in somatic rituals to DeMeter and other Black Stone Mountain Deities

- **rags of cloth** and **paper strips** sacrifices as simulacrum in Japan. In Ancient Greece and Africa, rags as sacrifices were tied to trees , and rags were tied onto tombs of saints from Constantinople to Cyprus to Syria and more. In Japan also iron wire dolls were clothed with rags and thrown into rivers as a sacrifice [17]

- **Spring Cleaning** sacrifices: see **rags** above and add England to this list as well for rag sacrifices and sweeping rituals occurring around March 3

- **Washing Day** (Laugar-dagr, loeverdag, loerdag) sacrifices: the name of this somatic ritual [18]

- **pole/post/tree** sacrifices: taking place *at the pole* has a double meaning, related to the Universe-Tree-Axis again, because its uppermost parts that connect to the Black Stone Mountain and its Polar Deities. There are a range of sacrifices here, made at stone pillars, stone columns, tree posts and poles, and even the Barber's Pole which was a sacrificial pole for bleeding out a victim of sacrifice, thus the red stripe on its design resembled blood that would drip down and splash upon it as blood was let.

In fact, etymology, as you'll read more in depth here, connects these sacrifices to the Black Stone Magnetic Mountain.

None of these things can be separated from **Black Madonnas** or even Madonnas in general due to the structural location of **Black Madonnas** Origin and the types of sacrifices made to Deities from this Celestial Zone.

Note about RED: The symbols in this book have been used worldwide by oral peoples, which makes them part of a broad usage, meaning they were not reserved for smaller groups. They have been a pervasive symbolic language, widespread and not only about color, but also about Cosmic order and structure, Divine Motion, Creation of the Cosmos and of the Earth, Milky Way beliefs…and part of these beliefs was that women having their period are *infertile* at the time, since their bodies were not saving blood for a fetus, and so they were kept away from crops and plants that were growing, and often just pushed away from the community during that time, accumulating the feelings that they are bad luck while having a period of time "devoid of fertility". Therefore Red would not be used to represent menstruation among all these other beliefs about the Cosmos, Cosmic truths and others of oral peoples. What was widespread and part of these beliefs were blood sacrifices give to the Highest of the High Deities, of which **Black Madonnas** and Black Stone Deities and other Polar Deities are.

So while groups of women did choose to honor their menstruation and its powers, this was not connected to the widespread beliefs and symbolic language and would only be used among people who were in agreement about it.

This was difficult for me personally to digest and it took some time for me to come to understand the beliefs around it, especially since at first I thought it was in contrast to all the rural magic based around Motherhood and the power of the Mother, but I was told this over and over no matter which rural area I visited, and I also told this by ethnologists in Italy, professional scholars, and community elders and the like.

SACRED MOTION OF THE COSMOS

Black Madonnas have a special role in the perpetual MOTION of the cosmos. MOTION is the Highest Supreme Divine Force in all the Universe for oral peoples around the world. So much so that they categorized and named their Divinities with specific etymological root words that denote these roles in keeping Divine Motion in order.

Circular/Round Dancing while singing songs of encoded Cosmic information, the Auguring of and performing circular movements around altars and making specific types of Sacrifices (the type of sacrifice and the type of Deity the sacrifice was made to) are all earthly efforts to both replicate and venerate this Divine Motion.

In fact, the taboo of being left-handed and of turning left or going to the left side, along with 'looking back at the place being left behind' originates with the belief that Cosmic motion perpetually turns to the Right…so that turning in the opposite direction is moving against Celestial Order or is the possibility of undoing the course of sacred natural movement. And while most cosmic motion is about revolving 'round, **Black Madonnas** are associated with the most unique aspect of Cosmic Motion.

===

The specific role **Black Madonnas** have in this perpetual Motion, this circular dance of stars, of sacred Cosmic MOTION of the entire Universe is: STILLNESS.

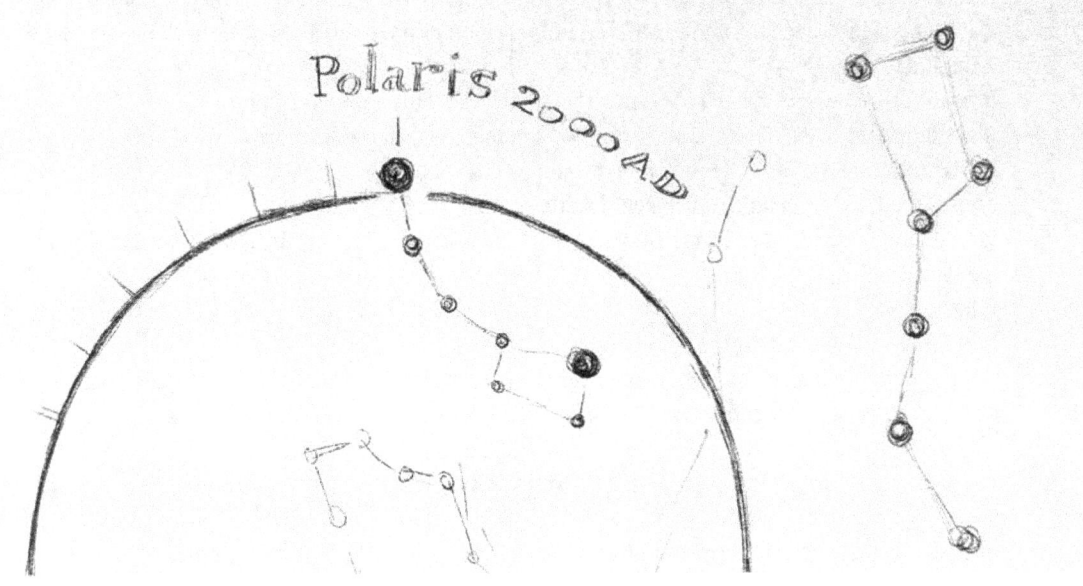

THE FORCE BEHIND COSMIC DIVINE MOTION

Why is this STILLNESS so important? The Celestial Polar North region and its Polestar are considered to be the Holiest, Highest most Supremely Divine region in the Cosmos. It's an especially unique region, inseparable from **Black Madonnas** and their role in celestial MOTION which is none other than: The MOTIONLESS Force that impels the entire Universe to move 'round it.

Many of the qualities attributed to **Black Madonnas** come from the qualities and attributes of this region:
- Stillness
- Sanctuary: There are many myths and folk stories about humans scaling the impossibly high Black Stone Mountain and being safe here ; reaching the Axis pole and holding on for safety because of a Universal Cosmic rule that anyone who succeeds in arriving here is safe to stay until moved by Deity
- Stability:The fact that the Mountain doesn't move yet urges everything around it to, keeping order
- Unwavering, Unswayable which is why the Universal Judges sit here in this neutral place
- Immovable power
- Neutrality, which is necessary to facilitate Universal Law, and why also Polar Divinities, like **Black Madonnas**, are considered Unconditionally Loving as in the case of Mamma Schiavona, and who also have to mete out Justice in the neutrality of the Universe
- Immortality, Eternal Presence (in myth, as an identifiable persona)

What power is behind this Force great enough to impel the entire Cosmos to move round its stillness?

A Black Magnetic Stone
+
A Black Magnetic Stone Mountain
THE SOURCE THAT DRIVES COSMIC MOTION

A Black Stone, magnetic, represented by a **Black Mountain** in myths which describe its power (because there are earthly parallels for all things existing in the Cosmos), this is the unique, powerful force honored as *Supreme Impeller of the Cosmos that makes the whole Universe move round*. This Black Stone is in the center of the Celestial Polar region of the fixed stars of Ursa Major and Ursa Minor and the Polestar.
- It is also the source of the Milky Way, often called the Heavens-River, and
- it sits atop the Celestial Crossroads from which the 4 cardinal points are drawn,
- it sits atop the Axis of the Universe-Tree and
- houses the Heavens-Palace and Arcana with Divine Secrets.
- It is the dwelling place of Black Stone Divinities and other Stone gods as well as the original Creator Deities.
- it has a Cave
- It is the area of the **Arg**os of myth, and
- the **Ag**ora marketplace of celestial space as well (the market of sacrifices and divine animals), the area of the *shining heavens* and *those who shine* …as well as the **The**oi, *those who see*.

Power of Etymology

Before delving deeper into the Black Stone, its powers in the cosmos and examples of Deities venerated as Black Stones, let's take a brief etymological journey into Root Words used globally to describe Black Stones as well as:

- Divinity names associated with it
- Celestial territory names associated with it
- Earthly parallels (locations and medicines)

These associations are necessary to learn about the Black Stone's Polar region so as to understand what is being communicated with these categorizations by root word. This will take us to one aspect of the TRUE NATURE of **Black Madonnas** according to oral peoples versus conceptual ideas that have been implanted upon **Black Madonnas** as committed by the literate world and that are disconnected from both Cosmic structure as well as nature.

===

Ag

One name given to the Great Black Stone Mountain of the Celestial Polar region is: **Ag**Dos. As to why will become apparent after this brief etymological unveiling attributed to John O'Neill and his work recovering this information from worldwide sources.
Ag is a word root, equivalent to: **Aj**, **Ak**, and even **Ax**

All have the same significance of: *Driving, to go*, to Urge, *to conduct the Universe.*
ay in Greek
aj in Sanskrit
az in Avestan
ago in Latin
again in midIrish
aka in oldNorse
ja in Etruscan (Janus)
and **ago**, the verb

Since **Ag** denotes: *to Drive, to Urge, to Conduct the Universe, the Impelling of the Universe...* when referring to a Deity it denotes: *One who Drives, who Urges the Divine Motion around the Black Stone Magnet, Conductor of the Cosmos...*

Ago, the verb, more primitively was: **Ax**im, **Ax**it, which etymologically connects **Ag** and the word **Ax**is both to the Celestial North Pole region, the Black Stone Mountain and the Universe-Tree-Mill-Axis, which oral peoples believed were vital components to this Cosmic structure: The **Ag**Dos atop the Universe-Tree-Axis pivot point around which the Universe turns.

All of these structures are important for understanding the role of **Black Madonnas** in Cosmic Motion, which will become more clear as we move along.

The Divine Force **within** the Black Stone Magnetic Mountain then, is its eternal immortality in relation to MOTION, being at the center of Celestial motion but remaining eternally Motionless.

Since **Ag**Dos is a Black Stone from which the Universe is **ag**ged round, the Deities found here also offer this type of Stability, Sanctuary and Neutrality in their approach to humanity. Found here are the Original Creator Deity Couples: The Old Man and Old Woman of the Mountain and Triad Deities, the Source of human souls as Divine Children.

Therefore the Stone Thrones of Stone Deities are also found here, which is what should be called to mind when viewing them in paintings of **Black Madonnas** and Madonnas generally. Deities which are in charge of this unique sacred MOTION of the Axis and surrounding Universe, the 12 Universal Judges who must be unmovable and unswayable by outside forces, also reside here.

Examples:

- DeMeter's Throne called **Age**Lastos on which DeMeter the Greek god-mother seated herself when worn out with seeking Persephone Night and day. There is a Well close by the Rock
- Another name is **Ag**Laos, the etymology of which we can see as: **Ag** denotes *impeller, mover, driver of Motion*; **Laos** denotes *stone*
- **Ag**Oraios was the Axis-column on which the whole machine turned [19]

The same Stone Thrones are found in Japan, China, Norway, Ireland…and so many more.

There are other Supreme Stone gods who are not Black Stone Deities, but the *Black Stone Meteorites, Aerolites, Natural Magnets* and **Ag** names are relevant to the origin of **Black Madonnas**. There is one other important category of Magnetic stones from the central heavens and which are prevalent in world-wide myths, which are the *loadstones*.

Etymology of Med-

While my next book will discuss Central Heavens Deities, it must be mentioned here the Deity **Me**Dea, who was a Stone Deity and venerated as a Black Stone though not a Polar Deity. In fact she was known as a Black stone named **Me**dea nigra [20]. She turned **Mag**nes (also called The Great One) into the Black Stone **Mag**net, and thus he was also venerated through a Black Stone. Therefore **Me**Dusa is also a Stone Deity from the Central Cosmic zone, though not a Polar Deity either.

Another important note about **Me**Dea is her connection with the number 12, which in this collection of beliefs refers to the Zodiac. Around the world the number of 12 stones was used in a circle, in the center of which was an altar to Deity. This physical emulation of a Celestial concept was emulated by Jesus and his 12 apostles but existed long before. **Me**Dea had 12 handmaidens, another note of Deities considered to be *supreme and of the Central Heavens*. [21] Her handmaidens were named Elikes, *meaning rotators as well as The Great Bear*, [22] which is their categorization of duty towards Divine Motion.

===

"The function of NATURE
is the Ultimate Truth for oral peoples." [23]

Below is a Brief list of Black Stones venerated as Deities from the Celestial Polar North, the zone of: Black Stone Mountain, 4 Cardinal Points, the Polestar, Ursa Major and Ursa Minor, the Top of the Universe-Axis-Tree, The Heaven's-Palace and place of Immortality.

This brief list is just meant to show that Black Stone Deities were not concentrated in only one village nor country. This list is not nearly exhaustive, and it contains mostly the Black Stones fallen from the Heavens…and venerated in their natural forms, before human-like impressions of Deities were carved into stones and wood.

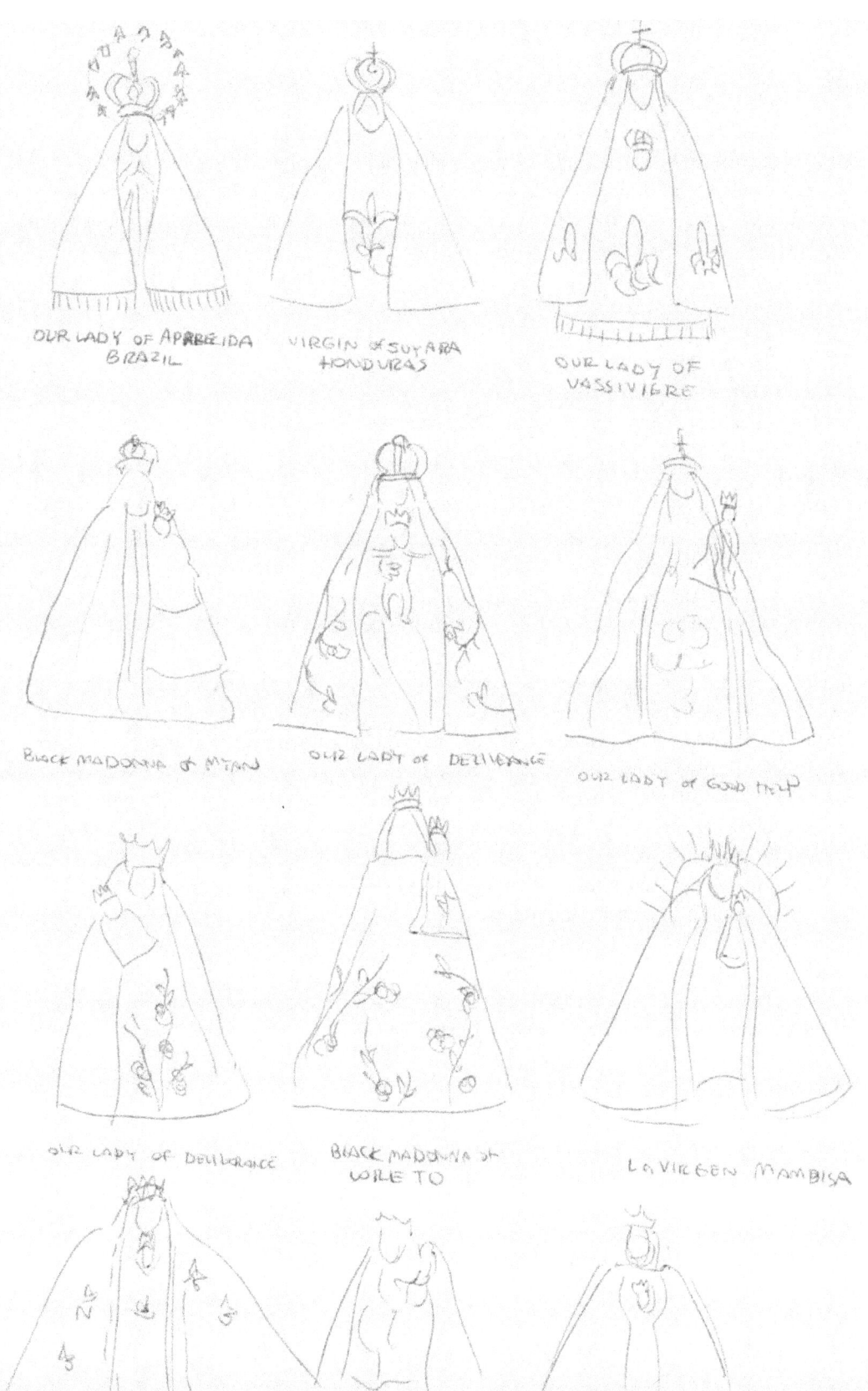

Note the Mountain-shape of the Black Madonna garments in these rough sketches of just a few of them

ITALY
- *Madonna della Sasso*, Madonna of the Stone
- Black river stones in Sicily carved with female breasts and genitals
- Black stones kissed by women before entering churches in the region of Liguria, Italy
- Romans would swear by Jupiter with a stone for Holiest of oaths, believing that this stone, Jupiter Lapis which was Black, was the Deity himself, whose name, according to their oath, *was neither Iu nor Iove nor even IuPiter bur rather Dispiter* [25]
- a variety of **Black Madonnas**

URUK
- 7 Black Stones of Uruk that were venerated as the 7 chief gods, the Mystic Great Ones from the Ursa Major / Big Bear. Gilgamesh was allegedly from Uruk, and here we also find the Ziggurat in 7 layers used as a ritualistic practice to ascend the 7 Celestial realms and spheres

IRELAND
- Ireland's Black Stone of the Swarthy Llyn Dur, Clogwyn Dur, and Maen Du Arduu near Lower Llanberris is a documented remnant of archaic stone worship of the Black Stone Mountain and Cosmic landscapes along with its mythic *Black lake*, *Black precipice*, near Lower Llanberris [26] and the Black stone known as *Black Pete*, a fallen stone Deity

FRANCE
- Students reported dressing up a Black stone with hats in a way that brings to mind stone rituals of swaddling, documented in Paris in May of 1453, as well as a report of the same hijinks with a Druidical stone. [27] The stones had "pet" names that were plays on the French word for stone, "pierre", so names like "Black Piete, devil pete". They actually took the stones on their own game-like procession through town and left them draped in herbs and cloths, which were found by the police. The report was written in a way that made it seem a known local custom, and the only reason the police were involved was because the students took this known stone from a woman's house without her permission
- 3 Black stones (Triad) fallen from Heaven, adored in the Temple of Chartres [28]
- an enormous variety of **Black Madonnas**

TURKIYE
- whirling Dervishes called *Rufai* and also the howling dervishes *kadiri* of Cyprus who wore a 12 pointed stone of contentment in the middle of their belts [29]

PHRYGIA
- Referred to as the Pessinous Stone, Black meteorite fallen from heaven which later was used for the face of a statue to Cybele, and then later covered with silver
- entire Mountain slope of Black irregular stones, all fallen from heaven

CENTRAL AMERICA
- primeval, animated obsidian stone of Goddess Citlalicue important in Mexican Creation myths [30]

AFRICA
- *Abbadires*, African stones as divinities, *baitulis*, means *powerful fathers*

EGYPT
- The extreme holiness of the natural Black magnet in Egypt, that is of magnetic iron-ore. It was said to come from Horus. So holy, that in fact non-magnetic iron was considered to be evil and belonged to the evil god Set. [31]
- *Abadir*, Semitic word means *great/glorious/venerable father*, title of Holy Stones called Betylus and also an alias for Jupiter who was also venerated through a Black stone.

SEMITIC
- Beth-Els/ Baetylia/ god-boxes: sacred stones instinct with Divinity in which the god was supposed to RESIDE and found almost all around the world. The Living Stone which is inhabited by a Divine Soul [32]
- Elohim are stone gods plural of Eloah, singular

SYRIA
- Stone of Emesa, as described by Herodios "Elagabalus..in the temple, a great stone, round at the base, pointed above, conical in form and Black in color, which they say fell from heaven" [33]
- [a meteorite] *Elah-gabal* the god of the Mountain, Mountain-El or Eloah. It was also covered with an enriched envelope, of metal, topped by a pointed crown. It was brought to Rome from Syria and then returned. [34]

ARABIA, pre-Islamic
- Al-**Lat** found at Symenat "an idol called **Lat** or al-**Lat** and was a single stone, 50 fathoms high, and stood in the centre of a temple supported by 56 pillars of massive gold". Al-**Lat**, in Mahomet's time was considered a daughter of the supreme god, who even earlier was the Mother of the Gods. This changing rank observed here is a continual process as to the newer divine generation ousting the older [35]

Her image at Taif was a square white rock which is now shattered by gunpowder but still laying *below the walls below the great mosque to the S.W. The names al-Lat and al-Ozza still survive for this rock and for the summit of the more southerly of the two eminences inside the town.*

All**at** is called *Lady of the Spear* in Babylonian records. Which brings together **Lat** and the spear, both are AXIS symbols, **Lat** is an etymological root word denoting: spear.

In fact, pillars in Orissa, India were common, along with the myth of Vishnu being associated with the Universe stone-pillar *having issued forth from the center of one* [36], and these Orissan pillars resemble Buddhist **Lat**s pillars which are also stone pillars. In Sumenat, India was found an idol called **Lat** and also al**Lat**. Pillar Deities commonly are depicted holding spears with Fleur-di-Lis or other Tri-tip symbols such as Tridents and other flowers with 3 points, petals or leaves.

SPAIN
- Our Lady of the Pillar (stone) of Zaragoza, Spain, which is one of the oldest Marian invocations

SAUDI ARABIA
- the Kaaba stone with its noted image of Aphrodite remains as shattered Black stone pieces set in a resin and silver showpiece shaped with vaginal reference. Housed on corner of a square structure which is dressed in Black fabric, around which Muslims must move in a circle *like the revolving stars round the pole, or the Black Stone Mountain in the Polar cosmic zone.* This is a cosmic replica of the Heavens-Palace on the Black Stone Mountain round which the stars turn.

GREECE
- A Black stone at Thespai was the most ancient and revered image of Eros
- Stone of Artemis called *manapasa* [38] had a metal bell-like cover similar to conical caps that represent the Mountain.
- Hermes: stone god, name from *Herma* = heap of stones. He's also an Axis Deity.
- the Petroma of Demeter: Arcadia oaths taken by this =2 large stones, inside the mystic books of Demeter were inscribed
- Black Holy Stone to which the Amazons prayed on the altar of Ares outside the roofless temple built of small stones.[39]

SYRIA
- Quaciou: one of chief gods of Aramean people, an aerolite Black stone, adored in many places as a Mountain God, common of stone gods. He was a heavens-fallen Conical stone In Syria, [40], also worshipped in Mt Casius on its summit in an open air altar and at Mt Casius where his idol was a figurative Young Man holding a pomegranate.

KINGDOM OF JORDAN
- A Black stone at Petra was worshipped by Nabatheans as Dhu Shera, Lord of Desire. Also of note: the Red Stone cut buildings with Pillars on the entrances called Rose City, with its most famous temple called Al Khazneh, said to date from around 300 B.C.

GERMANY
- suspension of many aerolites in German churches, widely known in the 1800s [41]

INDIA
- Orissa Legend of note : The Black Pagoda temple of Kanarak, has an Octagonal Black Pillar stone 50 yards high* [42] There were numerous shipwrecks near Kanarak and they were attributed to this "huge loadstone on the summit of the tower,"[43] meaning this earthly structure of Kanarak which emulates the Black Magnetic Mountain in Celestial space.
 - Black Stone + Tree Trunk worship in Orissa, India as well
- Lingam and Yoni Black stones in rivers.
*keeping in mind that 50 is the number of helpers needed for a soul to Ascend.

ARABIA
- loadstone myths of Celestial space told as adventures of Sinbad and Black Magnetic Mountain, where the Mountain is a mass of treasures and a great river of water runs into a dark grotto in the Mountain. This Black Mountain is an *aimant,* meaning alive with Spirit of Deity, and it traps ships because of their iron nails. On the summit of this mountain, which is very steep, is a dome of bronze upheld by columns of bronze topped by a statue who is the cause of the **magn**etism (the Deity itself) (See *la Varia di Palmi* in Chapter 2) [44]

CHALDEA
- The Deity *Gibil* was venerated as *God of the Black Stone* and worshipped on High Places. *Gibil* = Lofty Heights; the Semitic word *gabal* = Lofty, used to imply heights [45]
- Stone of Emesa, as described by Herodios "Elagabalus...in the temple, a great stone, round at the base, pointed above, conical in form and Black in color, which they say fell from heaven".
- *Elah-gabal* the god of the Mountain. [46], Mountain-El or Eloah. *A beth-El id sm El-dwelling, El-holder,*

(Starting left-right) 1. Aphrodite Stone, 2. Sicilian Carved Black river stone from Marija Gimbutas' "The Language of the Goddess", 3. Black Heavens-fallen Stone of Emessa, on a coin

and with beth-els can be found the junction of tree-worship with stone-worship.[47]

CELESTIAL HEAVENS-ROCK
- **Ag**Dos, the Black Stone Mountain rock situated as the Navel of the Cosmos upon which Attis sat [48] and from which stones were taken to Create humans and lands by Polar Deities.
- **Ag**eLastos, the Black Stone Mountain rock situated as the Navel of the Cosmos upon which DeMeter the god-mother sat, when exhausted from chasing after nights and days to find Persephone. Next to these rocks was a Celestial Well that reaches to the Earth.
- Black Stone of Heaven from which the Heavens-River (Milky Way) emanates

===

Comments on Black Madonna symbols found in their myths:

The symbols connected to **Black Madonnas**, and the Blackness itself, are directional signals that call is to Remember where she comes from and the unique Divine Motion she represents.

You should explore these myths, whether as rural folk tales and legends, or as church propaganda, and by the time you've finished reading this book, you will be enabled to notice what is encoded within some of them even if misinformation (by the literate folks writing things down) was added intentionally or accidentally. And, you'll be able to decipher even more mythic templates after reading my next book.

What we are being asked to remember in these myths: Nature is the truth and not human concepts of nature that have been derived in literate creativity and conceptualization *within the mind* as detached from nature. Myths tell stories of observed phenomena of the Cosmos and the resulting effects down on earth, as well as experienced spiritual phenomena which is always difficult to put into words.

So, if a statue *keeps moving itself somewhere,* back to where it was found (such as is common in **Black Madonna** myths) this story is a personification medium whose purpose is to get you to remember its origin by expressing it as *the preference of the icon* in a way your mind will retain. This *place it* *prefers* (whether on a stone, near a river, within a tree) is a Key Symbol to this Deity's powers (which are largely due to their Duty towards Divine Motion) and location within the Celestial Cosmic realms and zones.

Further, whether the statues are made of wood, stone, found buried in earth, etc, these materials do the same thing. They all call us to Remember: the Celestial Origin that each natural item denotes within Cosmic realms and zones: the Deity's access to earth. For example, are they an Ascended Master who can physically manifest on earth without having to be born as a baby and go through an entire embodied life again that requires a new body and memory-forgetting? What is their Duty towards Divine Motion?

These are vitally important ideas and symbols...not only for the Deities, but because they are implications for our own soul's abilities as we discover that we, too, are Divine Children (if we choose to discover this).

Short List of Black Madonnas, Key Symbols from their stories, and Country:

This extremely abbreviated list is not here to be an encyclopedia of **Black Madonnas**, but rather to show how the main symbols revealed in this book are a common thread within the mythic templates of **Black Madonnas** so that when you read them, you'll Remember.

SPAIN: Our Lady of the Pillar: stone pillar, Somatic Ritual with: Giants, dancing, Black

POLAND: Black Madonna / Our Lady of Czestochowa: Painted on cedar wood, her gown features a Fleur-de-lis. She is credited with saving a monastery during an invasion...this type of mythic template is connected to Madonnas and tree-top imagery more commonly, such as with *Madonna della Quercia* of Italy.

COSTA RICA: La Negrita / Our Lady of the Angels. Myth with all the relevant symbols: A lady was gathering wood near her house when she found a Black Madonna statue sitting on a rock. As she tried to bring the doll home, she would find them returned to the rock. Later, from the base of the rock, a source of sacred waters bubbled forth. [49] To discover why waters emanate from rocks, see chapter 3: WATERS.

NETHERLANDS: Our Lady of the Oak. Found in a tree, originally found by a farmer who took it home but it kept returning to the tree. Other stories say the statue was found in a river but kept placing itself in a tree. Her statue is made of wood. [50]

BRAZIL: Our Appeared Lady of the North *Nossa Senhora Aparecida do Norte*.
Fishermen found her statue in the river where they were fishing: first, her body, and just after, her head. Her veils have a Mountain shape.

VIENNA: The Black Madonna of Aloetting in Kaltenleutgeben. Her veils have a Mountain shape, her story is connected to a sacred well.

COLOMBIA: *Nuestra Señora del Rosario de las Lajas.* Her story contains rocks, water, a cave.

ITALY: 7 Sisters, each having a story with symbols from the Celestial Polar North (not the Pleiades which are impostors in this story). See details in my next book and in Chapter 6

General templates of icon discoveries: found on rock, made of wood, found in a cave, buried in the earth, in a tree, appeared on a pillar, next to a river, by a well. These are all mythic templates being used for remembrance.

===

Mag etymology and Magdala

There are *Heavens-Fallen Stones*, which are Meteorites / aerolites fallen from the Celestial Northern Pole and the Black Mountain, and on earth there are natural magnets. Along with loadstones, which are used to magnetize stones for the usage purpose in Compasses (which point to the Celestial Northern Pole), these are the Sacred Black Stone categories venerated as Deity themselves, and believed to come from the Highest High region in the cosmos, and are the Central Heavens Motion-Makers that move the Universe round…or, in the terrestrial versions, are parallels to the Great Black Magnet Mountain.

"Natural magnets of magnetic oxide of iron are sacrosanct symbols,
Holy Stones, dedicated to the worship and instinct with the Divinity of:
the Great Supreme,
The Great First,
the Uppermost,
the Polar centre of the Universe". [51]

Below are some meaningful treasures uncovered through the etymology go the word **MAGNET***
root: **magh** = to have power, power-possessing
mag, magh, mak = to be powerful

root of magh used in adjective form:
- **magnus** *Latin* = great
- **majus** *an old word for magnus* = great
- **magnalia** = wonders, grand actions,great things *in ecclesiastical Latin*
- **maha** *Sanskrit* = great, big, high
- **magus** and **maga** = a magician
- **magi** *Persian* and **magoi** *Greek* = great, to have power

Thus **mag**ic is simply and initially the exercise of the **mag** or power of the great central Deity [central referring to the Celestial North Pole region] and natural **mag**ic and natural **mag**netism get their sacred meaning from this region as connected by these root words.

The use of mag for roles or items:
- **Magister** = the Supreme, the director, conductor, ordinator, watcher, *over-see-r*, chief, master.
- **Magister** sacrorum = the high priest, the king of the sacrifices. The colleges of the Augurs [diviners] such as the Arvalii, Salii and Lares Augusti each had its magister.
- **Magada** = the name of the Venus goddess in Lower Saxony
- **Magodia** = religious mystery-plays
- **Magdalides** and **magdalia** = oblong cylinders.

Word components **mag** and **dala** from:
mag = great + **dallan** =the Irish diminutive and the name for the pillar-stones of Munster.
So then **MagDala** = great pillarstone (magnet + dallan)

- **Magnesia** = (the medicine) the powdered magnet used as a remedy in the middle ages, or later the drug milk of magnesia.
- **majus** = in low-Latin, was a tree, a *may* that is cut and planted as a sign of honour and worship

The use of mag for place-names:
- **Magdala** = a tower *in the older lexicons in Hebrew*
- **Magh-tuireadh =** the mythic plain of a mythic tower in Irish Myth. The Tower will be revealed as a symbol, on earth, of the Universal-Tree axis, as all round towers were built to resemble the axis.
- **Magnesia** = the mythic land of the Loadstone Mountain (Black Magnetic Mountain)

The use of mag for people names:
- **Magdala** = magnificent *in Syriac*

The use of mag for Deity names:
Magnes: was a mythological servant of **MeDe**a and changed by that goddess and sorceress into a Black Stone, The **Mag**net. His persona was thus wielded to the magnet's mysterious power, and so the magnet became divinely animated by [the consciousness of] **Mag**nes.
This also makes **MeDe**a a Stone Goddess (and **MeDu**sa as well)
Magnesia: title for the goddess Athene, which refers back to the Black Magnet Stone of power.

The use of mag for expressions:
"cuncta in **május** attollens" = *raising everything to a greater extent*

Other important connections:
So MAGNES, the masculine Deity name for the Black stone magnet , is the personal-name form of the adjective **mag**nus great and thus **mag**net reveals itself as the Great Stone. [52]

Additionally, his own father was **Aiolos**, that is, "*who causes Magnetic stones to fall from air and are also called aerolites*". Just to show here that etymology was used to categorize even the genealogy of Deities in celestial myths. [53]

The **mag**net is mentioned as ***an ugly and brown stone with which iron readily unites*** in a poem circa 1190 from Guyot de Provins. He describes how a needle, when touched with the loadstone and fixed in a straw or chip floating on the water, turns its point right against The Start that is, the Polestar.

The magnet is referred to as ***ugly and Black*** in many other citations. Note that the **mag**net was also considered powerful as it points to the Highest High Star and also guides sailors and land travelers.

Both the **mag**net and its Deity, **Mag**nes were referred to in this way in documented form in 400 A.D.:
"*The stone is called Magnes, discolored, dark, cheap*"
And **Maja**, the daughter of At**Las** (an Axis god whose name also means *stone*) and the mother of Hermes (a stone god whose name comes from *herma* = heap of stones) makes her an Axis-Deity as well…which connects us to *Our Lady of the Pillar*
Maium = month, Maja =goddess

34

Maius = god, so called from *greatness and Majesty*

*All this etymology collected from author researcher John O'Neill and has been added to.

Aside from this word journey being interesting, it's important because these words are related to celestial objects and personas that are used in symbolic form by oral peoples who venerated Black Stones as tangible pieces of the Highest Divinities in the Cosmos, or as tangible pieces of the Highest Divine Force of Motion in the Cosmos.

Painting of The Virgin of Suyapa by Karyn Crisis

====

SUMMARY

Black Madonnas, or the older Deities they have replaced, have a special role in the perpetual MOTION of the Cosmos, or, it can be said that they REPRESENT the most unique aspect of the Divine Motion of the Cosmos: the still, unmoving, stable presence of a Powerful Force (imagine a MOUNTAIN) that has a magnetic component that Impels (like a Director) the entire Universe to revolve round it.

Black Madonna icons are meant to remind us of the Divine Motion of Black Magnetic Mountain, and also express the attributes of the **Mag**net, which is honored in the month of May because May has an etymological root of **Mag**net. There are also Cosmic movements happening in May (see Chapter 9).

Black Madonnas are inseparable from Pillars, Tree Trunks and Tree Tops.

Black Madonnas are enthroned in the Highest of High places in the Cosmos and thus had blood sacrifices made to them. They are associated with the Black of the North, the White of the Heavens, as well as the Blue of Astral space waters in which the stars shine, the Red of sacrifices and Immortality, as well as with gold/bronze, a color I'm saving for my next book.

Black Madonna icons are often shaped, with their Veils, like Mountains. They are also literally Black stone or painted Black wood or terra cotta, they are carved from jet Black stones and meteorites, covered with celestial plants, and encoded with other Celestial Polar North symbols, including the Crescent of the Southern Hemisphere of the Milky Way (no, it's not a Moon Crescent).

OUR LADY OF U. HOLY OAK

OUR LADY OF HANDEL

VIRGIN MARY OF EINSIEDELN

COPY OF BLACK MADONNA OF LORETO & VIENNA

NOTRE DAME de la Sartre

OUR LADY OF LAGHET

GRACE OF THE BLACK MOTHER OF GOD

BLACK MADONNA OF SION

LITTLE BLACK IMAGE

BLACK VIRGIN (MOTHER OF GOD)

VIRGIN OF GUADALUPE OF FUENTERRABIA

THE MIRACLE MADONNA

Full page photo on facing page Credit: used with kind permission from Giancarlo Parisi, http://www.studioassociatoparisi.it

CHAPTER 2: NORTH

**The Polestar
and the Celestial Polar North**
Stella Maris
la Varia di Palmi
Madonna della Stella

...

Madonna of the star
where she resides
further on it doesn't go
My glorious image

Maria divine star
where she resides
further on it doesn't go

Please accept
thanks and favors
let us pray heartily to her
who can help us. [54]

===

Despite all my travels and meetings and stays in the rural villages of Italy and all I was taught there beginning in 2009 (though I'd been to Italy for business more than a decade before that) I had no interest in Madonnas for even a few years *after* that, not even realizing I'd chosen an Italian painting of a Black Madonna for my website background nor that I was emulating the Black Stone Mountain in atmospheric photos for my band Gospel of the Witches, nor aware of how many photos of Madonnas I'd taken in rural Italy and all the caves I visited hidden away on mountain peaks of various regions.

It would not be until I read through Italian rural prayers to Madonnas and Saints, and as I inherited more medico-magical secret words. It was then that threads woven together tugged at my awareness, and I felt the energy pulsing through them: first, through the secret words which I used regularly. Then, as I would translate prayers to various Madonnas from Mario Polia's fieldwork after interviewing him in a castle on a mountaintop in Leonessa: one in particular, where the Madonna was called also a **column** and a **ladder,** I felt so strongly, as if the words were alive. I knew something wonderful was happening through this prayer and energy was being channeled. And, as I said these prayers over others, they felt it palpably as well. At that point for me there was no denying conscious energy being turned on and channeled with these words.

I also noticed peculiarities in the form of softly mysterious double meanings of words and phrases also evident in rural medico-magical prayers for curing specific ailments. As time went on, I noticed rural prayers are very different from prayers released by the church online, for example, which until that time I had not examined. The communities utilizing oral healing methods keep silence on the meanings, while the church works hard to make explanations of the archaic symbols they use (the ones connected to Madonnas as well as ones the priests use), changing the script and leading us far away from the truth.

I didn't know anything about Madonnas nor mountains yet when I traveled across Italy interviewing people on mountain tops and down soft dirt roads in the countrysides and interviewed people for my first book in 2016, only that I loved Italian mountains: I was particularly entranced by the olive-covered ones of Valle Argentina in Liguria where it's easy to find herbs such as *iperico* and *strigonella*, and also of the lush and shadowy Monte Taburno in Campania where I saw *belladonna* and *datura* growing along with my favorite: *timo serpillo*, and that I seemed to have a growing reputation for being connected with mountains with each year I'd return there, because I kept receiving more and more invitations from people who would take me on 8 hour hikes exploring mountains in their regions with caves and tiny chapels on their peaks.

I also started noticing how many rivers were winding through Italy and how many were dedicated to Madonnas when a friend who lives in the mountainside village of Cazzocchia, Rieti, (I think 5-7 people live there and some only part-time) drove me through many tiny towns whose names I didn't catch while on my way through to visit other *piccoli borghi* with locals.

After these excursions, in my own meditations and work with my guides-in-spirit, I was being drawn closer to Madonnas and asked to combine images of mountains with herbs and forms of water: snow, dew, rain, and fog, not knowing that they had anything do to with Madonna della Stella nor the North Star. When I first read that prayer at the top of this chapter and the phrase: *non se va* "it doesn't go" lit., I could only conceptualize that it meant something like *no need to go further, I've found what I was looking for*.

It would be a couple years later still that I'd learn what it really was referring to: The Stone Mountain beyond the Celestial Pole Star that's so high it can't be seen from earth and is atop the Universe-Tree-Axis. This Mountain has been referred to as: **Tresmontaigne** and also **Tramontana** because it's said to be so High it's even above the Polestar and thus cannot be seen…in other words, *non se va* = 'can go no further, it doesn't go' in the Cosmos than this Black Magnet Stone Mountain and Star Light of Madonna della Stella, who is just one expression of **Black Madonnas**.

Celestial Polar North Particulars

-Star of the Sea
-Female Polar Divinity, Male Polar Divinity as separately operating beings
-Original Creators as Masculine and Feminine operating together as couple,
who create Divine Children
-7 Helpers: groups of 7 males, 7 females
- 4 cardinal points and 8 half-cardinal points
-Human sacrifices
-Gates of Heaven
-Heavens-Palace
-Celestial Black Stone Mountain
-Pivot of then Axis and Branches of the Universe-Axis-World-Tree
-Secrets of Divinities accessible to humans via plant elixirs : Soma, Houma, Graha

-12 Judges in Black Caps
-Cave
-Fleur de Lis, Lily, Pansy
-Pillars: single and double
-Stone thrones
-Celestial Crossroads
-Secrets within the Palace (**Arc**ana, **Arc**x, **Arc**h) such as:
sacred plants and Fruits from the Universe-Tree-Axis branches
-Deities are referred to with words like: The Great Extreme, The Supreme Rulers,
-The Motionless axe of the Universe around which all Motion Revolves, Sanctuary

===

In our contemporary literal expressions and phrases we might say this is the Highest place a soul can evolve to, working through the realms over thousands of incarnations, to achieve Oneness with the Universe…the Place of Immortality, but where it is possible to maintain some individual identity or of blending in with Source. The Black Stone Magnetic Mountain was envisioned as being a Mound that's so High its summit can't even be seen, and that there is no higher place in the Cosmos.

While the Black Stone Mountain and its **Mag**netism are the obviously significant aspects of the Celestial Polar North's particulars as related to **Black Madonnas** and Madonnas in general, the Polestar necessarily is as well and has been misconstrued under much misinformation, especially with the forced connection to the Pleiades.

The Polestar is part of the 7 stars of the Ursa Minor, and the 7 stars of Ursa Major reside in this Polar zone as well, rotating in a counter clockwise direction around the Polestar. Thus, these Bears (as the Ursas are referred to: Little Bear and Big Bear, each which contain the asterisms called Little Dipper and Big Dipper among other names) play an important part in worldwide Myths about assisting the Central Cosmic Northern Pole Deities and Functions. It's also an important locale regarding beliefs of the Original Creator Duo who created the Divine Child and are of Triad Deities.

"The Polestar puts all terrestrial things in order;
which, without ever ceasing,
produces and causes to be produced
animals and men." [55]

These stars are an exciting story in themselves, but for now we will focus on the aspect of the Star, which is the Star of the Sea, as related to the Madonnas.

Natural Magnets and magnetized metals created by Loadstones for use in compasses all point to the Celestial North Pole, and certain mechanical aspects of this zone are considered Fixed such as the Polestar itself and the Black **Mag**netic Stone Mountain, creating a stable, unwavering sanctuary. The stars dance around the Polestar, and its Deities have names, which, aside from titles expressing their Highest Celestial locales, refer to this stability, such as Dhruva which means **unshakeable**, **immovable**, or **fixed**.

In the photo above of The chapel of the Black Madonna in St. Peter's Basilica in Oirschot by Eline Kinsenbergen let your eyes be drawn to the Black Triangle of the Mountain. Underneath it in a glass tube is a carved wooden Madonna of Orischot, Our Lady of the Holy Oak. She holds a spear, reminding us that she is an Axis Deity with the ability to move up and down the Axis, and the glass tube is another reminder of this, imagine an elevator of sorts, accessible for Ascended Masters.
Used with permission. Https://www.facebook.com/eline.kinsbergen.9 ; from interfaithmary.net

===

The Polestar Deities are often called The Most High and The Supreme in general categorization. A few examples who use this term:
Ptah *Egypt* ; Magnes *Greece* ;   Amaterasu ;   *Japan* Akuti *India* ; Khaira-khan *Tartar* ; Tai-Ki *China* ; Athene Polias *Greece* ; Dhruva *Hindu* ; Anu *Chaldea* ; Attis *Phrygia* ; mi-Naka-nushi *Japan* ; Aengus *Ireland* ; Pohjantähti *Finnish* ; Hivel Zivo *Mesopotamia* ; Tuke *Anatolia* ; Aphrodite *Greece* ; Maat *Egypt* ; Ukko *Finnish* ; Janus *Etruscan* ; Sabazios Phrygia ; and Zeus Hypatos, Zeus Polios, Zeus Ep**Ak**rios *whose altars on high places were originally on the summit of a mountain* (486. Janus *Etruscan*. **Ya** etymology *to go*, see **Ag/Ak** in Chapter 1; and the 8th born of the 7 Kabirim *was a Polar goddess: The North Star* [56]

Being that they dwell here in what is considered the Center of Heaven as well as the Navel of Heaven, (and in parallel closer to earth, the center of the sky)*, the Polestar itself, as well as its Deities, have been symbolically worshipped on High places, such as altars or temples on summits of Mountains which replicate the Highest point in the Cosmos. This is a unique zone, a stable place in the midst of Cosmic Motion. *This belief has to do with Omphalos stones representing the Center of the World, wherever it is they are planted, as well as a voice-piece for Deities from this Cosmic zone.

Photo by Karyn Crisis, Napoli. Notice 4 Cardinal Directions and Triad symbols combined

THE Star, The Star of the *Cosmic* Sea

Why is the Madonna connected to Sea Farers, Sailors, and different types of waters?

The **Black Madonnas** and Madonnas in general have been connected to several aspects of Water in ways that other Deities within the Black Stone Worship beliefs are connected to:

- Walking on Waters: myths which are about achieving Immortality via Resurrection. Red robes are an indicator of this achievement along with indicating Human Sacrifices are required to this Deity
- The Moisture Principle of Creation
- Rivers due to the Milky Way aka the Heavens-River
- Navigation of waters via the Polestar shining from the space of Celestial Waters

Navigation of waters or land wouldn't be possible if the Polestar was in motion while being used as a guide. This makes it part of the unique Still, Sanctuary that the Black Magnetic Stone Mountain offers as well.

Note: these Waters are Celestial or of Celestial origin

With the **Black Madonna** being a personification of this High Celestial zone of the Black Magnetic Mountain, The Source of the Milky Way River, and an Original Creator Deity, her veneration as the Polestar is a natural one. Her connection to Sailors as a guiding light is expressed in rural stories and prayers to *Madonna de la Stella* across Italy. The mythic stories feature slight differences (regarding the water-weather feature mostly) using the same template, of the Madonna with child.

The Star, however, was not simply a *guiding light* in physical form nor conception. The Star's ability to Guide is in its stability, its fixed position as well as its relationship to the Black Magnetic Mountain which draws the Compass needle towards it, unfailingly. And, at the same time *The* Star, connected to the Blessed Virgin Mary, is a tool for those on the physical waters of the earth, but it is among the Celestial Waters of the sky, the Celestial Sea, Celestial Ocean, Celestial Rivers of astral, cosmic space.

There are many versions of the myth of *Madonna de la Stella* throughout Italy, but they basically say:

There was a dark and stormy night.
A young mother and her newborn baby find a ship about to set said from the coast
(insert Italian coastal town here) and asks for passage.
She is denied because the sailors say it's dangerous
due to all the fog that's preventing them to have a clear passage.
They worry for storms as well, and they don't want any harm to come to her or her baby.
There's one sailor who offers to give up his cabin to the young mother and child,
and he also gives her his flannel shirt, or in some stories it's a scarf...
and he stays with the other sailors.
The voyage begins, and there's so much fog and wind... but then unexpectedly,
the sky clears and the Polestar can be seen... it's bright and shining and
helps them find their way to their destination.

When the ship arrives and docks, there is a strange weather phenomena:
in some stories, it's summertime but they sailors find snow all over the ground.
In each story there is a water element: snow or fog or rain.
In the case of snow, the sailors notice small footprints leading across the land.
At the same time they notice the young mother and her child are nowhere to be found. They follow
the footprints in the snow and arrive at a statue of the Madonna with Child and the lent item (flannel
shirt or scarf= parallel to her Mantle) is wrapped around it... a sort of "thank you, it was me"
symbolic message.

Another rural prayer, collected and documented by Mario Polia, which expresses parallels drawn between the presence of the Star in both the Heavens and on Earth:

"Madonna of the star my advocate
that I come to see you in heaven and on earth
in this place where you are laid

*thank the night and the day ***
I do the grace and ask it
*So I ask you to make it to **me***

So please, Virgin Mary
I greet you and say avemaria." [57]

**notice Night is mentioned first, before Day.

Here, in a hymn to Mary called *Ave Maris Stella* allegedly from the 8th—10th centuries, the same connections are found. The "Always a virgin" line doesn't actually refer to physical virginity at all, but rather it is an expression of the separation of the Heavens and Earth.

"Hail star of the sea,	*Ave maris stella,*
Mother of God,	*Dei Mater alma,*
And always a virgin,	*Atque semper virgo,*
Happy heaven's gate"	*Felix coeli porta*

The name Maris Stella goes back to a translation of a book of biblical place-names by Eusebius, an important 4th-century historian of the Church. Jerome translated the Greek name Mariam into Latin as Stilla maris, "Drop of the sea." A later scribe, however, changed it to Stella maris, "Star of the sea," and from then on the term was associated with Mary as the guiding star through troubled waters. Churches by the sea have been named Maris Stella, and Mary is seen as the protector not only of sailors, but of anyone figuratively "at sea." [58] This is a documented example how how later (newer) cultures and writers, conceptualize the meanings of names, thus disconnecting them, as symbols, from their original knowledge and usage.

- The Subas, Sabaeans or as they call themselves the Mandoyo (meaning *ancients)* still worship the heavenly bodies and pray to the Polestar and put the sole door of their temple on the South side so that those who enter must face the Polestar, because their High Deity dwells there at its extremity. *"Sabaeans have no doubts their religion is older than Christianity, Judaism or Islam. A Sabaean house of prayer, which bears a cross[...] two branches of the olive tree [put on one another] making a plus sign, and the plus sign represents four sides of the universe".* [59]

- This Star is also likened to the Virgin Mary, the Madonna, in hymns, rural prayers, local "folk" stories and legends, among those who worship heavenly bodies, and even in other cultures who have "Virgin Birth" stories that express a very similar mythic template that Christianity created around its Divinities.

Some names for the Polestar:
- *tres-montaine, tresmontagne,* French [60]
- *clere Estoille de mer, qu'on nomme tresmointaine,* the Star of the Sea. *"Because therefore which part the point (of the needle) aims at, the tresmontaigne is there without doubt".* In these passages, the Virgin is addressed in the 13th century [61] as the Star as well as the Mountain.
- as: upright beam on which a roof rests, the king-post, socket *Arabic*
- as: the axle, the pole, the polar star
- *al nagmeh,* The Star *Arabic of Egypt*
- *Taivaannaula,* Nail of the sky *Finnish*

"In those parts below Tramontana
are the mountains of Calamita* that give the air the power
to draw iron; but because far away
you want to have help from such a **stone,** to make it of use,
and direct the needle towards the Star". [62]

*an interesting note is that Calamita is the name for Magnet in Italian, and it also means Calamus (root) and Reed, which are both symbols for the Universe-Axis. It's been posed that these are all connected due not only to the structure of the Universe (The Axis that connects with the Black Stone Mountain and is something Deities use to travel from earth to Cosmic space, but that also *the magnetic needle was put in a reed to float on water* [to act as a compass to find North].

Some names for the Compass
- needle of the pole, pole indicator *Arabic*: *ibreh el-kutbiyeh, kutb numa.*
- star-box *Chinese*
- in Europe and Arabia in the 12th and 13th centuries the needle was regarded as pointing to *the North Star, the motionless axe of the firmament*, to *the Star.* [63]

And some other cultural notes:
Female Polar Divinities with names related to Bright Light of the Star, such as *Pasi-Phae* (Greek) and *Amaterasu (Japanese)*, who are also associated with Birth and Resurrection in mythic templates. This also means that both Divinities are associated with the color Red: for human sacrifices and for resurrection.
- the Japanese legend recognizes Amaterasu existing before she was made sun-goddess. [64] She is part of a Triad Deity
- *Pasi-Phae's* name means *All -shine* and is mother of other Central Cosmic Deities, herself being part of the golden firmament
- There was an ancient Scandinavian order of knighthood of the Polar Star, which was revived in Sweden in 1748 [65]
- The Fleur-de-lis has been used Universally on the compass as that needle that points to The Star and also is the symbol of the Creator Deities that dwell there

Moving on to other symbols connected to the Celestial Polar North brings us to the Tree Pole as Ship Mast. This is referring to the Celestial ship of Resurrection that moves across the sky from West to East. Atop this Mast, such as with the Heavenly ship **Ar**go of the Bright Heavens, there is a Flag, which is an insignia of Authority: here, the authority of the Celestial Polar North wherein dwells:
- the 12 Judges in 12 Black caps
- Creator Deities
- Black Stone Deities and other Stone Deities
- Polar Deities…all of whom have a special relationship to the Divine Motion of the Universe through Stillness and Stability
- Triad Deities
- The Treasury
- The Heavens-Vault of the Mountain
- insignias of Authority such a: conical caps, flags, pillars, Fleur-de-Lis
- The Savior

These ideas are played out in the following ritual of Sicily that is still remembered today: Ntinna a mari, but first, another Somatic Ritual.

===

SOMATIC RITUAL OF THE NORTH
la Varia di Palmi

Credit: Used with kind permission from Alessio Marincola.

The *Varia di Palmi* is a Somatic Ritual of Calabria's city Palmi. Here, every 4 years a Procession takes place on the last Sunday of August in which a conical shaped float covered in silver and white, celebrating symbols of the Universe, specifically of the Celestial North Pole zone, moves through the city.

This Mountain-shaped float is carried on a wooden cart in Procession from the center of town that features a physical reenactment of the Celestial Polar North's Divine Motion of rotation of the stars *round* the Mountain and its Virgin Mary, here called *Animella* who is at the very pinnacle and from under her which emanate the 4 cardinal directions represented by 4 rotating angels. Her Mountain votive float is covered with flowers and plants, which are believed to have existed *first* in the Milky Way. Refer to Giancarlo Parisi's photo at the opening of this chapter and note the details.

The Procession of the Mountain, as a votive on a chariot as the Celestial Polar zone, is literally supported by the constellations of Ursa Major and Minor represented by the 5 groups of guilds who carry the Mountain on their shoulder, which has wonderful archaic symbolism being that it expressed the Celestial Polar and circumpolar structure, and the entire ritual celebrates the success of the Virgin Mary as Resurrected, an Ascended Master Madonna who survived death, known here also as Our Lady of the Sacred Letter *Madonna della Lettera*. There are also 12 apostles at the bottom of the Mountain which, pre-christianity, represent the Zodiacal 12 come down to earth.

The chariot structure is composed of an oak base, called *cippu*. The term *cippu* derives from the name given to the circular granite base with which the olives were ground. This is how the Universe-Axis is envisioned in many cultures: as part of a mill that has rotating segments and stationary segments. This chariot is carried upon the shoulders of men.

This Somatic Ritual is part of a network of "Celebration of big shoulder-borne processional structures"[66], carried by guilds of 5 classifications, and the origins of this somatic ritual date back to 1582. The guilds are called *mbuttaturi*, whose name means in dialect *bearers*, and, *to carry some load*. They wear Sailor outfits distinguished by colored scarves:

- *Artigiani* (Artisans) whose color is Red
- *Bovari* (Cattle Drivers), whose color is Orange
- *Carrettieri* (Cart Drivers), whose color is Yellow
- *Contadini* (Farmers), whose color is Green
- and *Marinai* (Sailors), whose color is Blue

The significance of shoulders in this ritual is archaic indeed and attributed to several uses of animal shoulders found around the world. In my book "Italian Magic: Secret Lives of Women" I relate how a sheep shoulder bone is used for divination in Sardegna as well as among shamanic groups, but divination by shoulder-blade bone is a worldwide custom, as well as is the sacrificial nature of that bone; meaning that this bone was used as a sacrificial knife as well.

The Egyptian *xepesh* demonstrates this within its own etymology as well as its usage. *Xepesh means: shoulder, fore-thigh specifically of the Ox, Ursa Major, royal blade, and power, strength. The god Mentu is depicted holding it. This knife is also mentioned in the funereal rituals as a northern constellation; and the leg-of-beef has given its name to the constellation of the Great Bear.* [67] The Zoroastrians called the Great Bear the leader of the stars in the North and the 2 other stars next to the polar in the Little Bear's tail were called the dancers. [68] Ultimately this sums up what processions like this are emulating: the turnings and the dancing of the stars around the Central Mountain point and Star.

But these uses and their significance all emanate from the Ursa Major and Ursa Minor (who are not envisioned as *bears* in every culture, but often as animals relevant to that culture) because it is these two constellations that revolve around the Polestar and the Black Mountain, while the last star in the tail of Ursa Minor is the Polestar itself. So these *rotators* are *bearers* in Cosmic Space, keeping the motion of the Cosmos turning and supporting the Black Magnetic Stone Mountain on their starry shoulders. And, these constellations resemble the shoulder bone of a bovine as well.

There are a few differing documentations about the quantity of bearers from the Guilds, and one report uses the number 50, which, in mythic templates, is the number of starry helpers that assist a soul in Ascension.[69]

And, as inseparable part of Processions, here also there are songs and music, specifically in this ritual from *taburinari*: frame drum players. The *palio*, which is twirled as the procession passes through the squares, is crimson red with the monogram "M" of the Madonna della Sacra Lettera". A Palio is a flag often won in a challenge or game. But the word **PAL**io refers etymologically to a stone spear.

Prior to this Procession is another one related to the Virgin Mary's hair. It is an historical reenactment of the arrival of the Sacred Hair by sea which takes place on the Friday preceding the *Varia* festival. This is none other than a Resurrection story of waters, which applies here to this particular mythic ritual about the Virgin Mary becoming an Ascended Master, rising with her physical body and soul to heaven.

The hair of the Virgin Mary was originally given to the town of Palmi in gratitude for the aid given during a plague to the Sicilian town of Messina, by the Senate of Messina in 1582. After which Palmi adopted the tradition of celebrating the Assumption of Mary with a votive chariot. Keeping in mind that the Ursa Major and Minor are also known as chariots in some cultures, as I discuss in my next book.

Symbols we see of the Black Magnetic Mountain of the Celestial Polar North in this ritual:
The Conical Mountain shape as Source of:
- flowers and plants
- 4 cardinal directions represented here by 4 angels
- on top of whom is the Virgin Mary
- chariot of oak wood beams (which I expand on in my next book)
- Shoulder carrying tradition (which is celestial)
- Sailor outfits (celestial waters crews)
- Resurrection myth and accompanying somatic ritual
- Colors of the Milky Way/Heavens River which emanates from the Mountain in the guilds
- Song and dance as a way of expressing the Harmony of the cosmic spheres and hidden insider knowledge
- Wheels (which I expand on in my next book)
- Ursa Major and Ursa Minor and the Polestar
- Zodiacal 12 (see Chapter 8)

What has survived here is a gorgeous Somatic Ritual acting out archaic beliefs of the revolving Universe-Tree-Axis and its Black Magnetic Mountain of the Celelstial Polar North.

===

Sicily's *Ntinna a mari*
"Antenna on the sea"
Night-to-Day and Balances
…Or, game of the mast of the **Ar**go ship, the heavens-boat.

In Cefalu, in the province of Palermo in Sicily, Italy, every August 6th a traditional Somatic Ritual expressed as a game takes place. It's called *'ntinna a mari* which is dialect for "Antenna on the sea". This game occurs on the last day of a patron saint's series of celebrations.

The game consists of:
- a wooden pole/ship mast that is extended horizontally from a ship and hanging over the water, like a "walk the plank" idea from pirate movies

- The pole is covered with a slick substance that makes it challenging to walk across it: grease or soap, or the like
- There is a flag affixed to the end of the pole, which is the focus for all contestants who try to walk, run, or stumble across the greasy pole to grasp it. The flag is often white (but also other colors like blue or yellow or a combination) and either has an image of jesus on it or is meant to represent the "holy savior". The participants have traditionally been the sons of the fishermen of Cefalu, numbering 17: 7 stars ofd Ursa Minor, 7 or Ursa Major and the 3 (Triad) divinity.

The wooden pole is the Universe-Tree-Axis. The grease, which it makes the game a Game for all the challenges it creates for contenders trying to capture the flag, is a part of ancient ritual to Deities from the North Celestial space called greasing the pole, where stones and tree trunks were anointed by oils to venerate Deities from the Celestial Polar North. [70]

The Flag is an insignia of Authority of the Polar zone. Like the **Pal**io in the la *Varia di Palmi* Procession, indicates a treasure won from the Highest Heights of heaven and the seizing of the flag recalls the exchange of balances in the myths about Ship Masts. These have 2 signifiers in this system of categorization:
1. One, the masts of celestial ships upon astral waters bear flags. Their flags are insignias of the authority of Divine Motion of Balance, turning of Night turning to Day.
2. Ship masts also represent the **Pal**, the spear that upholds the heavens Palace which as a center pole (refer to Native American ritual of *Man Eater* page 118) and are therefore another Axis giving access to the Black Stone Mountains Polar zones: the Treasury (which is robbed in myths) and other particulars where the Deities dwell.

The Mast of **Ar**goNavis (the Bright Heavens ship) is called Palladia Pinus, **Pal**=spear, stone pole..another Axis figure, and Pinus of the Pine Tree. All celestial ships and boats [see chapter 3] offer the possibility of Resurrection and Rebirth, navigating Souls through the Universe-Waters safely. In myth, the **Ar**go ship is further identified with the heavens by its mast which is an oak of the Dodona forest of Zeus, that is the Universe-Axis-tree, and it gives oracles. It is sailed to the Magnetic North Pole in the heavens of the *Theoi*, the Sky gods *who see*. [71]

===

MOISTURE PRINCIPLE
Venus Shell
TRIADS
Fleur-De-Lis, Lily and Pansy
THEOTOKOS

"springing forth the gods from Moisture..."[72]

Though Moisture is a water element, it is connected to the Celestial Polar North zone and the Black Magnetic Mountain due to its purpose in the Creation Story of Divine Motion, and because it's part of the Central Celestial Motion, it belongs here in our Celestial North zone. And, that all Waters emanate from Celestial space: the Black Stone Magnetic Mountain.

The Moisture Principle is the archaic belief that all waters emanate from ONE source in Celestial Space : The Black Stone Mountain, and thus various myths of water coming from rocks.

This *"original river is from the sky: the division takes place on the heights at the Pole, and the 4 resulting rivers are the chief streams of the circumpolar continent as they descend in different directions to the surrounding sea...Not only the Paradise [Celestial] rivers, but also all the rivers of the whole earth, have but one headspring and but one place of discharge."*[73] *"Even Plant-Sap, and blood, and milk and all the 17 kinds of liquid enumerated in the Yashts, are parts of the one cosmic current,"* and thus there are found Deities such as Akkadian "Mother of Rivers." [74]

===

What's interesting about The Madonna, the Virgin Mary, Venus, Aphrodite and the Sea Shell connection is: the one used in connection most often with them is a biValve called **Sun Ray Venus clam**. The reasons this is interesting are:

- The biValve, being 2 halves that separate, are almost mirror images of each other and which operate together to create an entire container for what's inside, and in fact, it's named after the Roman goddess Venus who is envisioned with 2 aspects often such as being the goddess of: the Night and the Morning, which feature in mythic templates about Balance.

- The biValve is an important Celestial symbol of Creation.
Moisture is considered a DIVINE MOTION. Archaically, worldwide, it is attributed to the Feminine principle, while fire is attributed to the Masculine principle.

- In India, this is expressed as the lingam and yoni stones found in rivers, the natural lingams a result of a meteorite colliding with the earth in the main river in which they are found, and the carved ones of Black stones, representing this as marking heavens on earth.

- There are 2 Deities, *bi* who are connected to this Moisture Principle of Creation: A Masculine one and a Feminine one, who were once united, making a 3rd container that housed the god as a whole, envisioned as: 2 heads, 2 sets of arms, 2 sets of legs, and both male genitals and female genitals.

- This being divided itself in 2, the original mutilation (later continued in Mythic Templates as Deities cutting off parts of themselves to create more Deities or in being mutilated by other Deities such as heads chopped off), and thus becoming 2 separate individuals. This is a Creation process for Deities and not for souls who become human beings.

- These duos are the Original Creator Deities: 2 coming from one, forming a whole that = 3: TRIADS. They perpetuate this genealogy through 1) Divine Children that are the result of 2) Mutilations (envisioned as: taking pieces of themselves to create new Deities, "chip off the ol' blocks). Divine Children are created when souls move into a zodiacal path in the ecliptic and move through the Galactic Gates into a physical body on earth. Mutilations are also a way Creator Deities create new Deities who don't go through the reincarnation and physical embodiment path.

- The Deity **Ag**Disits was one of these Original Deities who was divided i.e. mutilated by another Divine Being and then became: Cybele and Attis, an Original Creator Duo, a TRIAD. They create more Divine Children…Attis does this through mutilation, Cybele does this as Cosmo-creator who sends souls through the ecliptic and onto the earth plane. Thus the TRIAD is perpetuated.

Their more archaic names reflect these halves that were part of a whole:
- Axiokersa and Axiokersos -*Greek*
- Izanami, Izanagi-*Japanese*
- Tholad and Tholatha-*Phoenician* names of these principles, *Semitic* words

TRIADS often use the same name foundation for their offspring as well, such as with the TRIAD of: Kerement the father, Kerement the mother, Keremet the son. Perhaps the Christian story was emulating this with Mary, Joseph and Jesus.

The *keremet* (and other triplicate root word names) also all allude to their Duties towards Divine Motion. While the **Ax** names recall impellers of the **Ag** and **Ar** names of the Black Stone Mountain, *keremet* is the name given by Chuvash tribes near the Volga [75] to their sacred encolsures; their temples. The Mordvin Finns also have this *keremet* encolsure, and both are like the Mhadevi sacrificial ground of the Satapatha-Brahmana with is southern entrance (so entering one would face the NORTH Celestial Zone of the Deities connected) all 3 had its sacred tree in the center (as Universe-Tree-Axis is in the Cosmos, underneath the Black Magnetic Mountain) that is also its sacrificial post. The chief sacrificer would climb the tree, often an oak, *and conceal himself among the foliage* [76] which brings to mind *Madonna della Querica*, Madonna of the Oak (for more Tree Tops meanings see Chapter 4: Trees) as well as the Irish Divinities in their Rowan tree with its magical berries.[77]

The Finns placed their Great Bear in the top of the tree [78] (circumpolar constellation). Additionally, the Chuvash venerate Thor, whose hammer/mallet connects him to Mountain Deities, Thunder Deities (an element of meteorites, fallen pieces of the Black Magnetic Mountain made of iron oxide) and their symbols and place within the Cosmos.

Another example expressing a Triad is through the Great Triad of gods *of Zeus who governs the inerratic spheres and its revolution; Poseidon, also a Stone god, who presides over the planetary spheres and who perfects their prolific motions, and Plouton who is an Axis Deity who plunged himself into the earth,* [79] therefore also in Duty to the Motion rotation of the Axis anchored in the Mountain and a connection between the heavens and the earth. Aphrodite, who's been paired with Poseidon in the Moisture Principle Creation stories, was also called **Ax**iokersa and as such was depicted with a **Pal** (**Ax**is pole) on her head, which is a symbol of her power to create and her Duty towards Divine Motion, with a stone spear, by whipping up the element of water, first in celestial space, to then create matter such as land or even as souls who will pass through the ecliptic into a physical embodiment.

- the biValve is a symbol of the Separations of Heavens and Earth, commemorated in Polynesian myths and in the Somatic Rituals commemorating this belief with the celebration of the Ascent and Descent of the **Black Madonnas** from one chapel on high to the other lower in the village (see Chapter 9).

- It is also a symbol of the myths of the goddess being mutilated to form other Deities as well as other Cosmic Zones: *"Bel cut the goddess in 2 and so made the Heavens and Earth."* [80]

- It's the seashell connected to Aphrodite in art, and both Venus and Aphrodite are part of the Moisture Principle of Creation in the Cosmos, meaning they are envisioned to be Moisture Deities. Aphrodite is also named *Doritide*, whose etylmological root **Dor-** means a spear/pole/beam/timber, and is used in Deity names who are Creators and who use stone spears, for example, to whip up land masses from the ocean waters. This is another version of the Universe-Tree-Axis used in a specific way-rather than for travel, for Creation. Aphrodite was *Axiokersa* and as such was depicted with a **Pal** (Axis pole) on her head.

Moisture Deities are paired with Fire Deities, and the 2 together create through the mode of motion we call Heat. This sexual pair was often referred to as *twins* in myths…who then become separated. Inseparable from the seashell and the saltwater that the Venus clam is native to, is the Trident symbol of TRIAD Deities, who are Original Creator Duos who come from one, and then, after being separated, create more Divinities as "Divine Children". These twins, the Creator Duos are the: *Male and female principles which produce and reproduce all forms of nature,* [81], named as such in ancient representations.

Triads and Towers and Marriages of Nature

In an Irish legend, there are 3 sons of *Tuireann* whose name means Tower. (For this significance see the Mountain chapter). They get involved in a battle; they must fetch the 3 Apples of the Hisberna garden along with a Spear and other items that are all of a Polar Celestial Treasure substance and zone. Brigit is the mother of this TRIAD.

There are many sets of Deities who are marriages of elements that are from the Celestial North, as we are focusing on here:

HermAphrodite *herma*=heap of stones, Aphrodite-moisture and a Black Mountain Deity; marriage of Mountain stones and Water + their creations = TRIAD

El/Eloah +Asherah *El*=stone, *Ashera*= tree pole; stone +wood

AgDos Stone of the Black Magnetic Mountain and the **Well** right near it is another non-personified expression of this

And while often TRIAD Deities are portrayed as parents with a child: A Mother Deity, a Father Deity and a Divine Child, it's also common to find myths of 3 siblings such as in the Irish myth above and also in the Somatic Ritual of *ra Barca* from Baiardo, Italy. Also often in myths there are 3 males as a TRIAD Deity, or 3 females.

But where they all came from is a 3rd part: a whole that came from chaos and, after separating from it, introduced the first Law of the Universe: Order.

- Towers simply represent the Universe-Axis with widows at the top, indicating the Dwelling of the Original Creator Deities who are marked by these 4 windows which represent the 4 Cardinal Directions.

- What are meteorites and aerolites aka havens-fallen stones? Venerated is Highest Dieties, as **Black Madonnas**, and comprised of 90% and upwards of Iron oxide
- What do the Black Magentic Stone Mountain that **Black Madonna** Icons call us to Remember? Iron Oxide that is Magnetized and thus causes the entire Cosmos to move Round it while it remains still.
- What makes natural magnets point to the North? Iron.
- What symbol is Universally used on the compass to mark North? The Fleur-de-lis.
- What does the Black Stone Mountain draw to it, and trap in Loadstone myths? Iron
- What have gypsies used in attraction magic? Iron
- What color does are Iron oxide stones fallen from the Heavens? Black

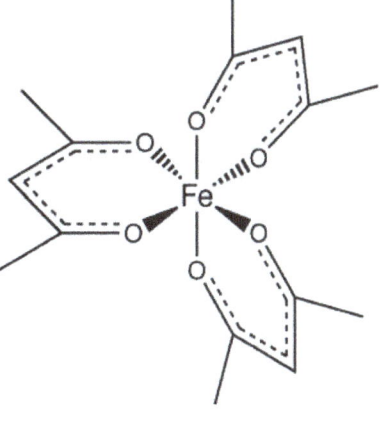

I took the photos above when my friend and writer Gianfranco Mele took me deep in the coutrysides of Sava and Manduria in Puglia. Here, down a long dirt road with old Messapian walls lined with wild herbs is this tiny structure, unlocked, with these wooden doors with a TRIAD symbol. Inside is this very worn Madonna painting. To bring full circle perhaps, notice the door pattern: it is none other than the structure of Iron Fe(34243), profane symbol of Highest of the High in Cosmic space.

===

**Fleur-De-Lis,
Lily and Pansy**

The TRIAD, TRIUNE, TRIDENT, TRI symbolism, though it may have been remodeled for propaganda about virginity and other social constructs around morality, were originally Arrows Pointing to the Cosmic realm of the Polestar and Black Mountain, its Deities, and the Divine Motion therein.

These symbols have been used on countless **Black Madonna** icons, on top of the spears of Deity statues once stone was carved into human form rather than just venerated in its natural form, and as tattooed on priests of Polar Deties. This is why priests of Attis had Fleur-De-lis* tattoos, because it was their Duty to protect the TRIAD. * Around the world, also, whether used in depictions of Deity, or even among human people in charge of others (like Emperors, etc), there are accessories denoting authority with the Fleur-de-lis upon them: crowns, tips of spears, gowns, other regalia, all emulating Deities such as Hermes, both a Stone Deity and an Axis Deity, who bears a 3 leafed-wand.

The Lily is another Triad symbol, and the Pansy is as well. These are symbols of the Highest of the High TRIAD Deities from the Celestial Polar North, the Original Creator Deities who spawn Divine

Children. See Mountain chapter for significance of the Pansy.

THEOTOKOS

One more brief etymological journey is called for here to uncover deeper secrets regarding one of the names given to the Madonna: Theotokos , which is said to mean "god-bearer" i.e. "Mother of God". **The** is also an etymological prefix used in Divine names by oral peoples for Categorization within the Cosmos of the Black Stone Mountain, meaning that this prefix was in use long before the church used it.

But where did this name come from?

A brief search says this name was given in the 5th century, after the council of Ephesus formally affirmed the Virgin Mary's status as Mother of God in 431 AD. However, Christiniaty's growth was due to the printing press which was used to create a united canon text around 1440 AD, noting that Chinese were printing before this, and used it to its advantage to implement a unified religion whereas before there were many christian sects, all ritual based, not text-based.

This is not the start of this prefix usage, however…**The** as a prefix was already used to denote:
- **THEOI** the Potent starry hosts of heaven
- **THEO** the movement of heavenly bodies, the ordinance and government of the universe (as a verb)
- **Theaomai** - to look upon, keep watch, control
- **THEO** -to send along similar to **Ag** aging round
- **Theuo** - to sacrifice, to burn incense, to be divinely frenzied

- as *The* **THEOI**: the Mighty, Lofty ones, pure, oracular, beneficent and powerful
- Ionic versions as verbs: running
- **THEA**- a goddess
- **Theao**-to show oneself, In its highest application referred to the Gorgeous self-display of the Supreme Heavens

Other meanings with the root **THE**:
- to see with wonder
- to wonder, revere
- a miracle
- to sacrifice
- to shake, move (Divine Motion)
- a sacrifice, a holy-day
- a victim (of sacrifice)
- Brightness

And the mythic **The**bes is the Heavens (not the ones on earth, which were built in parallel to the celestial **The**bes) is where we find the Treasury that's responsible for adjusting Balance : the Black and White changes: of day and night, the lengthening of night and shortening day, and vice versa…and of all the myths with Black and White sails, Black and White robes of Deities, Black and White sheep being exchanged between shepherds.

Thebes was claimed to be founded by Cabiric (Kabeiroi) goddesses who were interwoven in the Thebaic mythology, *Dionumoi **Theai***

THE and STONES
And at Thespiai, evidence of stone worship and temples for the stones which represented the god or goddess

* all of this THE etymology has been collected from author and researcher John O'Neill, and has had content added to it.

And that on the south slopes of the earthly Mount Pelion (there's a celestial one too) is a place called *Mavri-Petrais* (Black Stones) where nothing but shapeless stones [82]

Because of the **Black Madonnas** and their Origin in Black Stone Worship, it's worthy to bring just a couple examples of other Divine Beings categorized as "Goddesses" or "Great Mothers" so show their own connections to this prefix **The-**

DeMeter was known as **The**somophoros, the Lawbearer and that the temple of DeMeter interestingly housed a "statue of ProNomos the piper ." The pipe, the flute (also associated with Cybele's song and dance Processions) is a symbol of the Universe-Axis [83]

SUMMARY

Black Madonnas, or the previous Deities that **Black Madonnas** replaced, are **Theoi**: Bright-ones, Seers, Law-dispenser/Judges, a place of Unmoving Sanctuary, as the dispensers of Universal Law would need to be: unswayable, uncorruptable.

Black Madonnas are then also the Polestar, or it can even be said that the Fixed and always locatable Star, which draws **Mag**nets to it as the Black Stone Magnetic Mountain does as well, is always pointed to by stones from the Black Mountain, which **Black Madonnas** remind us to look towards in the Highest of the High Cosmic zone.

CHAPTER 3: WATERS

"Oral people mythologize history.
Literate people historicize myth.
For oral people, truth is Cosmic fact.
For literate people, truth is historical fact."[82]

===

WATERS
Walking On The Waters: Resurrection
2 Marys and Sarah
Madonna della Neve
and the Japanese Deity of Snow
Madonna de le Scentelle

The story of 3 Marys (or 2 Marys) and Sarah is told through a common Resurrection mythic template that has been used around the world by myth-makers and storytellers. As such, the creation of these templates by oral peoples, (and their celestial symbols, word prefixes/roots/suffixes used to categorize Deity based on duty to Cosmic Motion and Zone in the Universe) places its characters in an inseparable space from several other important symbols and zones:

-the Underworld of the Milky Way and the East (which is in the sky)
-Celestial Polar North
-The Northern Hemisphere of the Milky Way
-with Divine Triads and the Fleur-de-Lis
-With Universe-Tree-Axis Deities
Tree trunk-Axis Deities, Rooted-Axis Deities, and TreeTop-Axis Deities.

Painting from the 3rd century church at Dura-Europos, Syria, the Virgin Mary at a well.
Considered the Earliest image of Mary. [83]
This version painted by Karyn Crisis

61

The **Black Madonnas**, along with seemingly endless amounts of Madonnas and Marys have all been associated with WATERS. But, these Waters have different meanings based on where they are in Cosmic zones, and they have different abilities connected to them.These are expressed through mythic templates, often confused as alleged historical documentation. This chapter will shed a few points of light on a few types of waters and their meanings from an oral culture perspectives, but I will have to continue this explanation in other books because there exist separate categories for types of Waters and their support of Celestial Motion as well.

The main WATER categories in this chapter are:
- **Walking on Waters or Crossing the Waters**, as seen in the Story of 3 Marys and Sarah
- **Water Wells**, as seen in what has been called the earliest image of Mary from a Syrian tapestry
- **The Polestar** (that is in the Universe-Ocean) whose guiding light and **ma**gnetism is used by sailors navigating the Waters was briefly explored in the last chapter but needed to be mentioned here as connected to Waters
- **Rivers/Streams**, due to their parallel association with the Heavens-River aka the Milky Way and oral beliefs about its source and powers

===

WALKING ON THE WATERS

Mythic templates are standardized scripts containing universally understood symbols originating with oral cultures as a way of envisioning how the Celestial movements affect earth and keeping track of these relationships and that have layers of meanings (only some that seem obvious), that express very specific celestial occurrences that can also affect:

the earth
human beings
souls

These templates, by nature of their oral medium, exaggerate so as to be memorable. They are telling stories that take place in celestial spaces, along with any relevance for life on earth and those seeking Immortality or other secrets. Many of these meanings have been lost over time due to limitations belonging to the medium of writing and literate documentation.

In oral traditions, stories and myths and knowledge are Performed, creating layers upon layers of knowledge that each member of the group who is performing the Procession or other Somatic Ritual expresses. Writings can't encapsulate these layers and meanings (especially by outsiders) and instead conceptualize ideas about them...then each consecutive book or study or article only references other writings and eventually replaces meanings altogether through: erasure, rebuilding, and remodeling of literate cultures who then only reference written materials, missing all the information that exists outside of documentation...combined with the fact that as literate people, when referencing information in this way, we end up conceptualizing a great deal of ideas about things, not even realizing that in doing so we are disconnecting from nature and observance and experience of nature, which moves us further away from the bigger picture about life and death that was such an enormous part of life for humans....and a reminder here *that 99% of history has never been written down.*[84]

===

Mythic templates incorporate:

- a story that seems relatable to life-on-earth (though the landscape is Celestial and not earthly)
- a relatable figure or figures who end up on a journey that causes interactions with recognizable natural elements and locations which actually exist in celestial space but have parallels on earth…because oral peoples believed everything existed in the Cosmic space of Celestial Waters/ The Universe-Ocean first, and later earth was created
- wherein are villains and helpers : sometimes giant in stature, having only one eye, with outstanding weapons, who are described in symbolic ways that have to do with their Celestial zone location and relationship to Divine Motion and who are not earthly humans

-whose characters are challenged by some Force

that threatens their survival

or at least their well-being which is:

- overcome (=Resurrection)
- or results in a great fall after a disconnection of a vine or ladder (=Separation of Heavens and Earth)
- or results in a familial mutilation (of a child by a parent or of a parent by a child = a specific type of Divinity dividing its soul for new versions of itself to be reborn who can then move through the zodiacal ecliptic of 12 stages and options).

Historically these myths have featured, as their characters, alleged human figures of note for the time period such as Kings or Warriors, other spiritual figures called half-Deities, so as to be memorable especially in that time period, even if the character is actually a Divine being. Gilgamesh is an example of an historical King (well, his name was found on a King's list) whose epic astral journey takes place in this type of mythic template and who is considered also Divine. The Virgin Mary is an alleged human, whereas the Madonna is portrayed with abilities of a Divinity.

===

Regarding the Marys, Sarah, and their Water story, first let's boil down the following Water Resurrection myth to Cosmic symbolic basics so as to make it easier to catch the connected symbols and essential points of Cosmic truth. This is from French versions of the story.

Symbols found in these Water myths:

- **Waters** that must be crossed or entered or walked upon or survived in some way
- **Landscape** / mythic terrain that looks "earthly": caves, islands and the Underworld most notably. The Underworld is in the sky. Caves and islands are references to the Black Stone Mountain and Universe-Tree-Axis and Spear Divinities (of Triads)
- **Boats**
- **Characters** who must face a **challenge**: either a challenge in their journey or a physical issue
- **Divine intervention** by means of a Celestial Helper(s) who helps them make it across the waters: sometimes just one figure, at other times 7 dancers or 50 helpers
- **Journey to the East** or even the very far, Far East from the West.
- Some personal connection to Divinity: character has a Divine parent or gave birth to a Divine/partial Being

Comparisons to some other famous Water myths:

Both a spiritual figure and a constellation seen as a symbol of resurrection and eternal life, Orion walks on the waters and survives. Yes there are many other parts of the Orion myth which have to do with other celestial spaces and happenings, but here we'll examine the constellation's path and relevant mythic notes to Sarah and the 3 Marys:

ORION Walking on Waters

Orion was great hunter (1) in the underworld,
hunting Lepus the hare or Taurus the bull (2)
He walked on water (3) to an island (4),
He raped a celestial ruler there (5),
and was blinded in retaliation (6),
Orion was Guided by a divine Helper to the EAST uttermost East (7),
where he was healed when he looked upon the rays of the rising sun (8)
And was eventually killed by a scorpion bite(9)
He died, survived the Underworld, and became a constellation (10) in Immortality

1. In the sky Orion, as a constellation, is said to be poised hunting
2. The animals he is hunting in his mythic stories are constellations
3. This is the standard symbol of resurrection after dying and having achieved Immortality. The waters are astral space.
4. According to the oral Cosmic world, Islands are created by Original Creator Deities who have stone spears and are therefore Stone Deities (and may have other Deity abilities and associations). They spear a place…and whip up the celestial waters until a landmass is created (Japanese Onogoro) then mark its center with an omphalos…which is why, on earth, areas believed in each country to be "the center of the world" have an omphalos navel stone. The main element to be overcome in resurrection stories is always WATERS…because WATERS are the astral sky terrain, only survivable by SOULS who know the correct paths and correct passwords.
5. We don't know what was meant by rape, the context has been lost: perhaps one star colliding into another, but this is celestial. It is a behavior that is punished and therefore brings danger to him in the astral space, from which he is in danger of not returning to earth from, wherein he'd lose his physical body
6. Orion's injury will make his attempts to cross and survive the waters difficult, or impossible on his own…
7, 8. until he is divinely helped, and he's healed, meaning, he survives the waters arriving to the EAST where he is Resurrected
9. It is the scorpion bite that indicates he is moving through the proper celestial gate (of Scorpio) to achieve immortality
10. His immortalization is commemorated in the stars, as a as a Constellation forever known as it walks the waters (i.e. celestial space the sky) to remind us eternally

Celestial Movements

Removing all extraneous parts of this tale, and getting to the essential myth template which tells a Celestial truth: Orion, the constellation, appears to be Walking on the Waters with the **Ar**go ship* taking the same path: moving from the West (the realm of death) and rising, or being Reborn/ Resurrected in the East.... Technically, Orion appears to set due west because of the rotation of the Earth. This constellation lies along the celestial equator and, as the earth rotates on its Universe-Tree-Axis, it always rises due east and sets due west. These Waters are of course the Universe-Ocean, i.e. the Sky

*(**Ar**/**Ag**/**Ak** related to Celestial North Pole, specifically the Black Stone Magnetic Mountain and the Argo ship is from Argos, the Bright Heavens)

**The EAST is where celestial bodies rise, and therefore where all Deities arrive/return.

- Orion could walk on the waves because of his father : Orion was the son of the sea-god Poseidon. It's important to note that Poseidon, in earlier days, was not believed to be "god of the oceans" but rather god of the Celestial Ocean / the Universe Ocean, as well as part of a Deity Triad that is associated with the Polestar region...and that the earthly connection to waters comes later, because of the the belief that earth was created after all things were created in celestial space. This perspective offers important insight into the Walking on Water myth templates....and as with all myths, they are expressing movements and occurrences on Celestial time, not on earthly-time nor on earthly lands.

- Orion fathered 50 sons, and 50 is the magical mythical number of helpers needed to by a person who is dying and attempting to ascend to Immortality on that last epic journey of the soul's climb to the highest realm, as discovered by John Knight Lundwall.

- Boat on the waters: the Celestial boat, sometimes as a constellation in this case the ship **Ar**go (another one is Canopus), that crosses the waters and helps a mythical figure to cross the waters safely in the face of challenges. This is all astral. The crossing of "one side of the waters to another" is for example, setting in the West (death possibility) and rising in the East (reborn).

- Celestial Waters = An Astral Journey

===

Gilgamesh Walking on Waters
Boiling this myth down to Cosmic basics:

Gilgamesh and a friend go on journey (1),
his friend kills the bull of heaven (2),
and is punished by the Goddess Inanna and killed (3),
Gilgamesh goes to island (4),
in search of secrets of rebirth to try and resurrect his friend
who has died on their adventures.
These secrets are in the Underworld (The Challenge 5)
and to get there, he has the impossible task
of crossing the impassable waters of death and surviving (6) (because he is
a human going into a part of the Cosmos reserved for spirit people
to request help from a Divine Being who
is the only human who survives this task named: Utnapishtim. (7)
Gilgamesh is Divinely helped by 50 celestial helpers who sparkle in the sky
and are led by 7 helpers (8)
and crossed the waters in a boat (9)

The Epic of Gilgamesh is documented in writing in 1900 B.C, and oral tradition goes back at least another 1000 years. [85]

1. The characters begin their journey
2. Actions are taken which must have consequences
3. Punishment is received
4 Gilgamesh begins his otherworldly astral journey to acquire the secrets of life
5. The Challenge is laid out
6. The Challenge is impossible to survive as an embodied human
7. He seeks a semi-Divine being: the only human to survive this Challenge
8. Gilgamesh is saved by Divine Intervention: though he has "died" i.e., passed out of the physical world, he is being guided to Immortality by the 50 helpers.
9. He crosses the waters in a celestial boat and arises in the East.

- Gilgamesh, as King of Uruk has great significance in the Black Mountain Divinities stories, since in Uruk is a place of Celestial Markers on Earth that replicate Cosmic spaces, and on earth, was considered one one the most important cities at one time in ancient Mesopotamia. It boasts the architectural achievement of Ziggurats, 7 layered structures that were built so humans beings could practice ascending the 7 realms. Each layer of the ziggurat had a color related to the Celestial sphere/ realm it was emulating. Here also are found 7 Black stones venerated as the 7 Divine Beings of the Polar Zone's Ursa constellations.

- Gilgamesh was envisioned semi-Divine like Orion, a Divine Child-turned Immortal figure. Technically, Divine Children must discover their Divinity through physically embodied earth lives, so Gilgamesh would then, according to archaic beliefs, been created from the Original Creator Duo, then sent through the ecliptic zodiac to take on enough soul-expanding physical lives that would help him acquire knowledge for ascension to the highest realms.

==

Herakles Walking on Waters

Herakles has a similar journey, that of 12 Labors (1):
Through a deep, rocky cave,
Herakles made his way down to the Underworld (2) and
meets his first Labors, or challenges, with success.
Then he encounters Cerberus, attempting to take the 3 headed creature (3) with him,
and he succeeds at this impossible task.
Herakles had 50 Helpers (4) who helped him ascend to the Highest Immortal realms
to ultimately triumph over all the Labors set forth to him as challenges that seemed impossible for a
human to overcome.
In the end, Herakles released Cerberus
so it can continue its Duties of guarding the gateway in the Underworld.

Herakles began this labor by being initiated into the Eleusinian Mysteries. Then Hermes led him down into the Underworld. Note: Hermes is both a STONE god and an AXIS god...using the Axis here in myth for travel.

1. The 12 Labors represent the 12 zodiacal phases of humanity, the ecliptic.

2. Herakles began this labor by being initiated into the Eleusinian Mysteries. Then Hermes led him down into the Underworld. Note: Hermes is both a STONE god and an AXIS god...using the Axis here in myth for travel.

3. Herakles overcomes all his Labors/Challenges which take place in the astral realm, and are set up to make any human fail.

4. Cerberus originally had 50 heads, according to Dr John Knight Lundwall who discovered this in his research along with the 50 Helpers that exist in all mythic cultures, said to "sparkle in the sky," and whose purpose it is to assist a soul with Ascension into the highest realm. So, Cerberus is an envisioned representation of the 50 sparkling Helpers.

===

Iason/Jason and the **Ar**gonauts has a similar story..and many more do round the world.

===

Jesus Walking on Waters

There are also several stories about Jesus walking on water. The odd thing about these water stories though, is that Jesus is portrayed as the guy who puts 12 others in danger and then saves them. So he's not, himself, going on any type of quests nor facing danger. Instead, it seems we are seeing the perspective, in these myths, of the savior, rather than of the person facing death but achieving immortality and divine status. Scholars have claimed that these myths are indeed Resurrection stories, which then turned into baptism rituals.

Myths Combined from Matthew and Mark chapters in the bible:

Allegedly Jesus had been talking to a large crowd of people.
After he finished his talk and sent the crowd away, he sent **12*** men,
which are called "his disciples" into a boat on the water (1).
He went up on the mountain by Himself to pray, day turned to night
which left the 12 men in the boat in danger (2)
(3) the boat was being tormented by the waves and the men could not help themselves.
On the 4th night of the watch, Jesus was the Divine Intervention they needed,
as he walked across the waters (4)
(an inference that they were in the astral waters and dead)
to the boat and made the sea calm down (6)
then Jesus helped the men cross over to the land in the East (7), resurrecting them.

===

2 Marys and Sarah Walking on Waters
which truly should be worded as "the TRIAD"

For this myth, there are 2 exciting sides to examine:
1. the Mythic story and
2. the Somatic Remembrance

Mythic story
The myth of the 2 Marys and Sarah crossing the waters faces the same types of challenges all

myths face when examined from an historical perspective: a wide variety of dates (and no way to prove them), a wide variety of debates on whether Sarah was a servant or a noblewoman or a daughter of one of the Marys (and no way to prove it); a wide variety of allegations of which Marys were the ones in the boat (and no way to prove this), whether the people in the boat were fleeing persecution versus various stories alleging about how they ended up in a boat (with or without other people in the boat and no way to prove them). There are debates about the churches built in France where this myth takes place and when. The debates go deeper still, especially from testimonies within the village where it takes place and among different participants. For example, there are a lot of people alleging one thing or another about the gypsies connected to this, but where are the testimonies fro the gypsies themselves, especially the oldest ones?

There are, however, common symbols used in all water mythic templates, and these symbols (the archaic ones) tie them altogether towards core beliefs about the Cosmos pre-literacy, so we'll focus on those, since they are also from the Origin of the **Black Madonnas**. The dramas themselves i.e. the dangers, the perils, and the outcome are also symbolic parts of the myths structure:

The myth of Three Marys and Sarah says:
- The Marys were forced onto a boat that needed cross waters to the East/ to safety, which seemed impossible due to circumstance.
- Yet due to Divine Intervention they are saved, and this story has quite a few variances.
- There are wildly varying dates attached to this story, for examples, as well as varied landing towns.
- There are challenges: The boat has no sails, no oars, so they are adrift and there are dangers on the waters such as storms, not to mention persecution they left behind on land (in some stories).
- Additionally, some stories say Sarah was not with them, or that Sarah climbed onto another boat and helped the Marys come along, or that she floated over to the Marys in their boat on her clothing, which she threw on the waters…and safely helped them arrive to the East.
- Everyone makes it safely to "the other side of the waters".

But to PROPERLY see this myth, let's organize a bit:
The 3 Marys (1) were in some kind of danger (persecution, fleeing..) (2) forced onto a boat (3) More danger: the boat's oars had been taken away so the women were forced to be in the open sea without any means of helping themselves (4) Sarah comes along (5) and offers Divine Intervention: she throws her clothing on the waters and reaches them or helps them reach her in another boat by walking on her Fabric/clothing (6) They reach the EAST arriving on the others side of the waters (7) (coming from the west. The east is where the boat was pointed to at the beginning of the myth. They all survive the astral waters and return to earth (8) by landing on the EAST land.

In some versions, Mary **Mag**dalene is named as one of the ladies in this story, which is significant, because in addition to Sarah's **Blackness** reference and her statue that stands on a **Black** stone, the name **Mag**dalene is directly connected to the Black Magnetic Stone Mountain that Black Stone Deities come from. MAG root is magic and connected to **Mag**netism of Black STONE at center of Cosmos and Underworld. There's also a source of water in the site where the church was built and there's a sacred well nearby, which is a replica of the sacred Cosmic well near the Cosmic Mountain.

Important comments about Sarah:
- Sarah-the-Black is one of the names Sarah is called by. This name is direct as it can be, reminding us of the Black Magnetic Stone Mountain a the Center of the Cosmos.

- Sarah as a noblewoman: Keeping in mind as well that the Celestial Polar North was considered the Highest of the High, or holy, to peoples, so Sarah's identification as a noble person would be a tool of remembrance for this. Whether Sarah was a human being who actually existed, and whose name was put into a Mythic Template in a parallel situation for the purpose of remembrance, or whether she was a non-physically embodied High Celestial Deity of the Black Mountain, the idea of royalty applies here. From flags, to treasures, to Fleur-de-lis insignia, all the symbols that are used by human rulers and royalty are symbols that point to the same idea in Celestial space, and it's the humans who are emulating this Cosmic Authority.
- Sarah and Gypsies. As far as Gypsy connections with Sarah the Black generally, while this is not a personal report, there are many documented ethnological writings about Gypsies using loadstones (as well as other energy-healers like Mesmer) for a variety of rituals, spells and potions, either worn just as the natural stone in a pocket, or as *ground up into powder swallowed in ardent spirits ay bedtime while a magic rhyme* [with encoded-meanings] *is repeated about: 3 Black kids, 3 Black cheeses and the loadstone.* Some of these Gypsy usages are similar to Southeast Asia's Malay courage stone, and love potions and healing remedies from other cultures. [86]
- Sarah's clothing. Throwing clothes on the waters is a sacrifice simulacrum. See **Rags** further down

...The Somatic remembrance of this myth:

May 24

The Shrines containing the relics of the Marys are lowered [see Chapter 7 for more details about Separation of the Heavens and Earth] during songs and dances. The statue of Sarah is led in Procession to the sea, carried by the Gypsies, of whom Sarah is the Patron Saint. There is a symbolic expectation of the Marys.

May 25

The boat (replicating the Celestial Boat for souls) containing the statues of the 2 Marys is carried out to sea in a procession. After blessings, the procession returns to the church in joy (of the symbolic reconnection of the Heavens and Earth) and there is more singing and dancing.

This movement of taking icons *from above* and then *down* to another place and then back *up again* is a Somatic Ritual acting out the Mythic Template about the Separations of the Heavens and Earth. Each one is a little different, telling a story of reuniting, or telling a story of Celestial line-up of Cosmic events that are envisioned as these High Divinities coming back down to earth in a special way that must occur due to the original separation. Representatives of these Deities are often people immortalized in mythic story, as well as in statuary that has a Somatic performance aspect for these ancient traditions.

The **wooden** statue of Sarah is layered with fabric, layer upon layers of veils that, when they become too many, are taken off and this begins again. This is also a Somatic Ritual of Remembrance.

That a church was built housing the icons on a spot that allegedly found a natural spring appear, and that a well was built here are examples of bringing the Heavens down to Earth to emulate the sacred waters of the Cosmos which emanate from the Black Stone Magnetic Mountain. This site was also allegedly previously used to venerate Mithras and other non-christian Deities.

"She stands on a Black rock, swathed with tapestries" [87] .
Watercolor of Sarah by Karyn Crisis

===

OTHER Deities INJECTED into versions of this myth:

- **Kali (+ etymology) kar**, later **kal** = to go, to drive. This root word comes from the same etymology as **Ag**, **Ak**, **Ar**, the very Black Sone Magnetic Mountain we keep referring to in this book, and is also related to pole / pal / stake. [88] Therefore the root word of Kali's name reveals why she's depicted as Black.

- **Kali + Durga** Celestial Northern Deities who received appropriate scarifies for being so, such as: *foot-long effigies of a man made of dried milk for Durga and Kali pujahs*, [89] which is a simulacrum for human sacrifices. This is done by old families in the sect of the Vamacharis. *In the eastern district of Bengal this is frequent; and the milk-man is actually stabbed and hacked to pieces secretly at midnight by all the grown-up members of the family.* [90] This is a reenactment of Divine Mutilation, which would thereby create new Deities. Therefore the root word of Kali's name reveals why she's depicted as Black

- **Astarte** Astarte is associated with an Aerolite, that is, a **mag**netic meteor that was observed falling to earth, accompanied by thunder*, and many of these aerolites observed falling from the heavens to earth with flames and thunder have historically been attributed to Polar Deities and believed to be representations of this, such as the Mother of Gods, as well as some to male gods. Meteorites are believed to come from the Heavens-Black Mountain and fall from there to earth, while natural magnets point there and Loadstones can turn stones into magnets as long as they contain unactivated iron. *significance of Thunder: inseparable from stones falling from heaven as it is believed a s sort of announcement for the stone and part of the stone's animation, that is, that it is imbued with soul/spirit of a Thunder-Mountain Stone Deity and accompanied by lightning often. *Pietre fulmine,* that is, Lightning-stones also known as thunder stones in rural Italy are another oral peoples amulet, used for protection.

Photo of Conical Caps by Karyn Crisis in Trieste, Italy. Dome-shaped hats,
Conical caps are reminding us of the Mountain.

- **Aphrodite and Astoreth** Both are also associated not only with WATERS but also with Black Conical Stones (Mountain shape) that have fallen from heaven. The Black Stone Heavenly Mountain also features a cave: one in the Northern Milky Way Hemisphere and one in the Southern Milky Way Hemisphere.

- **Artemis** was venerated through a naturally Conical (Mountain) shaped Black stone that fell from heaven at Ephesus, a location known for worship of the Great Mother Goddess in various forms.

- **Mary MAGdalene** (Magnificent Stone Pillar), The meaning of "**Mag**Dala" as The Great Pillar, brings us to another mythical memory personified and embedded in myth…Our Lady of the Pillar of Spain. (see Chapter 5)

- **Ishtar/ Istar/** associations of importance with older beliefs about the Highest Celestial Zone of Cosmos, she a Deity of:
- revolving heavens. These sphere symbols unfortunately have been confused with SUN symbols, causing so much misinformation. Heavenly Spheres are often what people call "Sun discs", but in truth Sun worship came much later than worship of the Heavenly Spheres (realms)…and was forced into previously established beliefs which didn't even consider the sun nor the moon as part of the important Cosmic zone. In fact, while beliefs about the Milky Way are consistent throughout cultures round the world, beliefs about the sun and the moon and when they came into existence vary wildly.

A Babylonian prayer: *"Oh Lady Istar, Queen of the Universe-Mountain, goodly stronghold of the Mountains, mighty lock of the Mountains; Queen of the Land of 4 Rivers"*[91]
*reference to the 4 Cardinal Directions that emanate from under the Celestial Mountain.

An Akkadian and Assyrian hymn to Istar begins: *"Though who as the AXIS *of the Heavens dawnest, in the dwellings of the earth her name revolves."* [92] *reminding us the Axis is connected to the Black Stone Mountain and gives Ascended Masters not only the ability to move the entire cosmos round with it (since all stars and matter and space are envisioned as being connected to it) but also it's a means for them to return to earth and then back to the Heavens.

But most interesting, perhaps is Sarah's connection to Clothing: layers upon layers of clothing that are placed upon her icon statue, the Clothing in her Myth with the Marys, story, and the reminder of the tradition of clothing-wrapped stones as well as the man-made structures of: wood poles held up by heaps of stones (Hermes, from herma=heap of stones, who is also an Axis Deity) placed in a conical pile resembling the Mountain, and the rags tied to the top of the poles as as Sacrifice simulacrum (substitute for blood sacrifices) to Polar Deities connected with the Black Stone Mountain. That would make Sarah the Divine Intervention force who saves the Marys and resurrects them.

Which then also brings us to:
Mother of the Rags

Rags in short…are a devotional human sacrifice simulacrum to Tree Top/Universe-Axis/Black Stone Mountain Deities. Throwing clothing on the waters is a simulacrum as well, used in places beyond the myth of Marys and Sarah: such as in the list of Blood-Sacrifice substitutions in Chapter 1, along with "Washing Day" purification rituals round the world where dolls dressed in rags of clothing are thrown into rivers.

In Rieti near Lazio sinking into the side of the road are the remains of a church *la chiesa di san Vittorino*, built on top of a pagan temple that features a water source in its interior…which has since been reclaimed by nature.
Photos by Karyn Crisis

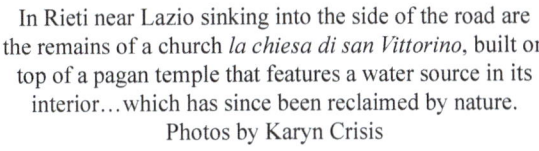

In addition to the briefly mentioned Tibetan and Korean version of heaps of stones holding up a tree post whose upper branches are decorated with rags of fabric, which express veneration to the Spirit of the Black Stone Mountain, *A tamarisk tree called the Mother of Rags, Um-esh-sharamat near Suez in Egypt has been observed covered with rags of clothing.* [93] This is a naturally constructed version of the personified Sarah's wooden statue version: a tree with rags upon it, the Tree being the Axis rooted into the earth as well as to the upper heavens, where Polar Deities dwell.

Some other lovely examples are:

"Throughout Constantinople, on the windows of the tombs of saints, pieces of rags are tied and called nezr/vows. Rag offerings of shred from raiment still hang on the sacred trees, and the tombs of Moslem saints in Syria, and tombs in Cyprus" [94]

"Irish peasants, to this day, cover the trees and bushes at sacred spots particularly near a sacred well with threads and scraps." [95]

"In the Egyptian desert the trunk of an old tree, or a pole secured in a heap of stones, and ornamented with old rags, each pilgrim who passes adding a rag to it." [96]

"The custom of placing ex-voto offerings, generally pieces torn from the garments, on or near the tomb of a holy person, prevails throughout the East. Frequently the branches of a neighboring tree, and the iron grating of the windows of the resting-place of a saint, are completely covered with such relics."

And in Celestial replication of Marking the Heavens on Earth...in Akra, near Ghana, the burial ground near the fountain was made gay by the many-colored shreds and remnants of old garments which fluttered like streamers from the tall headstones." [97]
(remembering that **Ak** is a root of the Mountain who makes the Universe turn)

RAGS then are connected to Water Rituals from this Black Stone Mountain belief system as well as to Sweeping cleansing rituals, to healing/scapegoat/ex-voto propitiation, Axis veneration, to Tree Deities veneration (various parts of the tree and Various Duties towards Divine Motion) as well as pilgrimages and rituals which involve moving 'round the pillar, 'round the tree trunk, 'round an upright stone... emulating the stars dancing round the axis and its Mountain.

===

WATER FROM ROCKS

"The Japanese Heavens-River is a broad, peaceful, stony bed,
the River of 8*, with its separations near the pole...the Milky Way" [98]
*8 being used to designate the half-Cardinal Directions.

From the myth of Moses saying that he struck a rock from which water flowed forth abundantly, to the many Madonnas of various waters (snow, rivers, rain, fog...and the magical Dew of 100 Flowers Water of rural Italy), there's a reason for these stories: the archaic belief that ALL waters emanate from the Black Stone Mountain of the Milky Way...that is, the celestial waters, the Waters of creation of the Creator Duo and their Moisture Principle that births all life, the waters (and all its forms) that emanate from the Black Stone in the Highest Polar Cosmic zone...and all these waters trickle down onto earth as well. So that waters are not terrestrial in source but Celestial. This is also why so many temples built near wells or around natural springs, and even churches adopted this symbolic expression of the powers of water by building churches next to wells, water sources, and the route to them: Axis, the Tree.

-Bhavani, Parvat or Ganga, consort of supreme Hindu Deity (as Siva), is queen of Himala and she sends fecund waters in all directions, having been born from the head of her father, king of Mountains, in the form of the boiling spring of the divine river which falls from the heavens upon the earth" [99]

Artemis Potamia was...regarded at Olympia (another mystical mythical Mountain) chiefly as the goddess of rivers, lakes and floods: and this makes a Central Heavens-River goddess of her." Floods have to do with Creation and the Separation of the of Heavens and Earth. [100]

In Mexico where *Tlaloc*, the god of the Waters dwells, in the North on the highest mountains, whence come the rains and all streams." [101]

Egeria was a Heavens-River goddess before becoming a terrestrial perennial fountain. The meaning of *Egeria*: E-gero=to bring forth or forward, she was also a Heavens-Mountain goddess. [102]

The Irish *Boyne* is called after the goddess *Boann*, and the Shannon after the goddess Sinann, and both rivers suddenly burst forth from the sacred or the secret well. They are manifestly Heavens-rivers, as may also be seen from the Brugh or Heavens-palace being on the Broad-Boyne. [103]

Japanese Cosmic *Mount Kagu* brings together in its myths: stones, waters, snow, Polar Deities, Bright-

Shining, thunder, mallets/hammers and meteorites, and Original Creator Duo couples who also create city centers on earth marking their epicenters with Stone Spears (representing the Universe-Axis); the Highest of High Deities, and Divine Triads as well as Somatic Rituals for sacrifice stand-ins along with color associations with metallics of the Highest Heavens. Kagutsuchi produced the 8 Mountain-gods, from when his father mutilated him into 3 pieces and created a TRIAD of gods:

- Ida-dzuchi, the great hammer, god of Thunder
- O Yama tau mi, the Great /Old Mountain and
- Taka O Kami, the High great god, the god of rain, snow, and storms.[104]

==

Madonna della Neve
Madonna de le Scentelle
Madonna della Stella

-MADONNA OF THE SNOW

The Madonna of the Snow, whose local legends are remarkably similar to Madonna of the Star, is most simply an expression of a Polar Deity who is Immortal, who is an Original Creator Deity who dwells beyond the Heavens Gate enthroned in the Heavens-Palace within the Black Stone Magnetic Mountain, from which the:

- 4 cardinal points emanate…
- and from where all waters emanate, both Celestial waters and terrestrial waters and all the fluids

- *Madonna della Neve* then, is a Polar Deity. From the Cosmic Polar zone.
- *Madonna della Sasso* is a stone Deity from the Black Stone Mountain.
- *Madonna de le Scentelle*…that is Madonna of the Springs, is also a Polar Deity of the Heavens-River, or the broader Milky Way. All of these Madonnas, including **Black Madonnas**, are used as seasonal expressions of water, sometimes interchangeable and have locations next to each other such as in Umbria:

Somatic Ritual: Pilgrimage to the *Madonna de la Scentelle.*
On the first Sunday of **July,** from the villages of the *Val di Narco*, people went on a pilgrimage to the *Madonna de la Scentelle*. The pilgrimage was followed by an agape consumed on the lawn in front of the little church, irrigated by a small stream. According to an ancient tradition, witches once gathered around the little church. In dialect, *scentelle* is a spring of water that gushes. The *Fonte de le Scentelle* is near the *Madonna delle Stella*, and rhymes have been written about its icy water.[105]

Somatic Ritual: Pilgrimage to Madonna della Stella in September together with the harvest, the threshing, the shucking of the corn and the pilgrimage to the *Madonna delle Stella*…recalls the songs of the girls intertwining between the rows of the vines.[106]

Somatic Ritual: The feast of the *Madonna della Stella* in May, the first Sunday. From testimony, *"there is Mount Maggio that acts as a lookout for the largest mountain that is there. Further down there is a fork, all the people must spend that month there because they renew the feast of the Madonna de la Stella."*. [107]

Somatic Ritual: *The pilgrimage to the Sanctuary of the Madonna della Stella took place on the **first***

*Sunday of May. The first to leave for the pilgrimage were the inhabitants of Roccatamburo, the closest to the sanctuary, then those of Rochetta, then the others. From **Trivio** di Monteleone, the pilgrimage headed towards Nempe, passed through the "**forchette** D'usigni", reached Poggiodomo and **descended to** the sanctuary. In addition to the devotion, the occasion was propitious for meetings between boys and girls of **engagement age** and also represented a moment of happy conviviality since, after the pilgrimage, people would rest near the **waterfall** adjacent to the church, a hearty breakfast would be consumed on the grass, people would meet up, they would sing.*[108]

* Note that this last Somatic Ritual stars from above and then descends…which is a reenactment of the joining of the Heavens with the Earth (see Chapter 9 for more Processional Rituals on this theme).

SUMMARY

Black Madonnas, or the Polar Deities they replaced, remind us that from their Celestial epicenter, the Black Stone Mountain, all waters emanate…which is why over time, many goddesses and female divinities, younger versions who replaced the older versions were named to represent the forms of water.

Black Madonnas have also succeeded, as souls, in Walking on the Waters, which is to survive the astral journey through Celestial waters and, rather than incarnate again, resurrect into an Immortal Ascended Master. In order to achieve this, **Black Madonnas** souls must go Under the World into the Underworld (The Milky Way's Southern Hemisphere) in Celestial space, and then, with the Help of 50 sparkling Beings, Ascend to the Northern Hemisphere of the Milky Way.

Black Madonnas should therefore be remembered as Orion is: a constellation who reminds us of Resurrection through the seeming disappearance of light in the west and its resurrection or rebirth in the east.

CHAPTER 4: TREES

THE VIRGIN SWALLOWING OAK
The Universe-Tree-Axis

Stories are many, of Madonna figurines reemerging after being swallowed by the earth, or discovered seemingly being disgorged from the trunk of a tree that had swallowed it up long ago. I've seen some gorgeous photos of intentionally-made tree-shrines in France that are filled with dozens of Marian icons all the way up the trunk and filling the boughs. This is a common theme in local legends about people finding icons as well such as: a chicken was pecking the ground and uncovered a Virgin Mary statue. These stories are the marks of Myth and beg the question, *which came first, the chicken or the egg?* as to the intention of it all...are these phenomenon created in glorious synchronicity by the Madonna's spirit, or were they intentionally created for the purpose of remembering knowledge of the past?

Even as I was working on this book, or rather had taken a break from working
on this book, I was walking down a familiar street, about to take a left turn onto another street I've
tread over and over in my neighborhood. I felt something touch my hair lightly and reached up to find
nothing there. Then it happened again, on a super windy day, but this time I thought I heard a small
rustling sound, quickly looked up and saw a crow flying away, low. I'd always had a great rapport
with crows, so I was concerned in this moment and took a sharp left turn, hoping to not repeat this
when I almost walked into a small tree trunk that, on this day, had a plastic Madonna patch hanging
from it! I walk by this tree almost daily, and it had never been there before. (images above) This I took
as encouragement to keep working, keep writing, keep searching!

Being *swallowed up by the earth* and *swallowed up by trees only to emerge once again* are in fact oral Mythic Templates of the worldwide Black Stone worship beliefs belonging to the category of the Universe-Tree, specifically of its stem, referred to as The Axis. Other parts of the Tree will be dealt with in my next book. These myths are kept in circulation and in Somatic practice to keep the knowledge alive, as is so often found, beyond the time of oral cultures. These local stories all bear the same template:

- on a farm field, a chicken begins to peck and uncovers an icon of the Madonna;
- someone hid an icon in a tree during the war. The tree grew around it and later it reemerged through holes in the trunk;
- someone finds a statue and it's too heavy to move;
- someone is in a cave and sees some blue flames and decides to dig and finds an icon;
- an icon was found near water, like a river, and then placed into a tree. Whenever it would be moved elsewhere, it would be found back in the tree or back in the river;

Then…

- hereafter being extracted, the human experiences some connection with the Madonna or with a Bright Light that feels like the Madonna, reinforcing that connection can be made with Divinity through this icon, which is usually:
- carved from wood or painted on wood or made from stone, a natural progression from venerating Deity through natural stones and trees
- the finder of the icon is compelled to construct a temple at the site of its recovery /discovery

These mythic templates, whether for Tree trunks here (there are ones for Tree Tops as well, such as *Madonna della Quercia*) or Mountains, are memorable stories that are trying to do just that: remind us of the Deity's relationship to Divine Motion, i.e. the Deity's powers and dwelling locale in the Cosmos. There is an allusion, in every myth, to the icons *moving themselves*, i.e. having consciousness and preferences and the ability to physically change places. Being personified in this way, they are easy to repeat, even long after the layers of original information they contain are forgotten.

You've perhaps already noticed, before opening this book, among local stories and myths, that Madonnas are associated with a selection of natural items, such as: Trees and Wood, Black Stones and stony formations, Caves, Pillars and Water…Ivy and Roses… All of these items, for oral peoples, are Cosmic and all the local stories and myths allude to their Cosmic Origin as well as their Cosmic Locales. There's more to the story than simply a gorgeous statue being found and inciting inspiration or miracles.

A few of these Mythic Templates:

Osiris, *Egyptian*: Whose dead body is found in the trunk of a tree *which had grown 'round it.* In the papyrus of *Har-si-esi*, Osiris is called *the one in the tree.* [109]

Druope, *Greek*: Druope's myth is interesting because it portrays her as already being a Divine persona who is then transformed into another type of Deity…or better said, she is made to go through another Divine transformation which acquires her new Deity abilities and duties towards Divine Motion: She was already envisioned as being able to gift Crowns and Wreaths, which are reserved only for Deities who've acquired them, as they are a symbol of Eternal Time itself: a circle of time, and a symbol of supremacy.

Through myth we are told:
-Druope was gifting Crowns of time/Wreaths of time to nymphs*
-She notices the lotus flowers at this lake and decides to pluck a lotus for her baby, but she forgets to ask permission of the plants.

80

-As a result, the lotus doesn't have time to withdraw its energy and
is injured by the plucking: it sheds a drop of blood,**
then begins to tremble with anger at its injury.
-This frightens Druope and she tries to run away.
-As punishment, the lotus makes Druope's feet grow into the ground,
affixing her in place. Once she's firmly rooted,
the bark of the plant she has injured suddenly *engulfs* her,
wrapping her entire body within it, as she thus becomes a Lotus Tree herself.

As a result, Druope*** now has Axis abilities that allow her to engage *in a physical way* with the earth, being that she is rooted here, *but she also has travel abilities*, represented by the Tree Trunk that she becomes, which are abilities assigned to Ascended Masters. This makes her not simply a Fixed Axis-Tree goddess, but a *"rooted Universe-Axis-Tree goddess"* [110] *just like Daphne.*

Important note here: all types of Celestial mutilations in myths resulted in the Creation of new Divinities: father chopping up a son, mother killing child, etc. This is a Milky-Way specific process and these myths are found in all cultures. Compare this Creation story against souls taking 1 of 12 potential paths through the zodiac via the ecliptic into a physically embodied human experience as a Divine Child who may yet discover this divinity through thousands of incarnations on earth.

*nymphs are not earth-dwellers, as people mistakenly believe about myths, but have a very High Duty in Creation of the Universe and with duties towards very specific elements of Divine Motion.

**blood drops in these mythic templates also represent the seeds or beginnings of new Deities.

***The spelling of *Druope's* name has since been changed to *Dryope* which disconnects the name from its original etymology which cuts it off from its history, sadly. The original etymology is needed in order to understand Cosmic zone and Duty of *Druope*.

Daphne, *Greek*: The myth of *The disappearance of Daphne in a tree-bole* is that "the Earth opened and *engulfed* her, and a daphne-shrub sprang up," [111] after which she became a Universe-Tree-Axis. Being an Axis, which is a structure that, while it moves the entire Cosmos 'round the Black Stone Mountain and Polestar and is connected to the entire Cosmos, is also envisioned as a stable structure, insofar as it is doing the "moving round" while everything attached to it is moving 'round with it. This is why Daphne was also remembered in Somatic Ritual in a round/circular dance and why the Daphne tree-stem is grasped, in other myths such as with Apollo, for stability.

Oedipus, *Greek, Egyptian*: Oedipus, also called Oidipous as well as *Swellfoot* [112], was the mythical king of Celestial Thebes, that is, of the Heavens. This technical nickname can be likened to the Fomorian Giant of Irish myth called *Sotal of the Big Heels*. Feet deformities, in myths, are about Axis Deities that are rooted. Imagine that gout, or a swollen heel or oversized gnarled foot is like the root of a tree, deeply pushed into the earth.

Oidipous is turned into an Axis Deity when he meets his end
'being swallowed up by the Earth,
while sitting on a stone-throne [of the Heavens],
where the way parts into many roads [113] i.e.
under the Black Stone Mountain where the 4 Cardinal points emanate from.

In fact, Oidipous lived at the Universe-Pillar at the hill, or mountain side, which is *why he was also named Oidipous Koloneous/Coloneous/Colonel (from Greek spelling =hill, Kolonis connected to columen and columna and column.* [114] Interestingly also, for our **Madonnas** connection, in addition to the Column and Pillar connection, there is a fountain named after him, like the Well located near **Ag**Los. He murders his father, is the consort of his Mother who destroys herself after in a particular way…all of these actions of mutilation and death are telling a Cosmic story of Deity-creation and are not about earthly incest.

Attis, *Phrygian*: The body of Attis was *enclosed* in a pine tree until spring. [114] Attis is also a Divine Child like Oidipus and thus has mutilation as part of his story.

AtLas *Greek*: AtLas, buried deep in the bowels of the earth by Kronos, and who, as a Pillar-Axis, supports both Earth and the Heavens. From here, he had access to the Highest Heights as well as the low earth. AtLas' name indicates his mechanical connection to Divine Motion and his ability to travel between Cosmic zones and the earth: "The current Polestar, at the very end of the tail of Ursa Minor, has names in various languages that mean *Axis, socket, axle,* and *pole of the Universe* (as in, connected-to). From this *pole* it is envisioned: AtLas sat **Las**=pole, diligently investigating subterranean and celestial affairs […] by whose all-piercing Eye the depths of every sea are clearly seen; and who the lofty **pillars** strenuous rears, which every way divide the Earth from the heavens".
Laas =stone , Stone Deity names with **Laos, Las, las,** AtLas of the stone pillar [115]

Indra, *Hindu, India* is described the same way in the Rig Veda "*Indra, who has upheld the earth and heaven and the firmament.*" [116]

　　　　Both of these Divine Beings are often described as having their heads touch the Pole and their feet resting on earth and their bodies like slender mountains, so tall that their summits are out of sight and, who because of height and being Fixed like a Tree Trunk (Axis), are likened also to Pillars. Pillars are envisioned as a stationary support mechanism of the Polestar holding the rotating universe together. The Axis technically turns round, rotating while it spins the Cosmos, but it does not set nor rise nor change shape. Hermes uses the Axis to travel and is also a Stone Deity among others. Similar such Deities are:
- Samoan *Ti-iti-i*, Polynesian *Ru*, Greek *IphiKratos* and *Magnes* [117] and
- Egyptian *Shu*: In the Harris Magic Papyrus (ii,3,5) *Shu upholds the heavens, which Anhur then brings-round with his spear (Axis). Shu is the stable, Anhur the turning,*[118] [together they create the] forces of the Cosmos.

To add a scientific note that relates to the Stability of the Axis and the way oral people envision it connected to Divine Motion of the Cosmos: "*a spinning gyrostat whose spinning-Axis is compelled by the experimenter into a horizontal plane, is then constrained by the Earth's motion along to direct its spinning-Axis due N and S and so to indicate mathematically the lie of the true meridian of its spot. If the spinning gyrostat be next shut-off from all other motions except a VERTICAL one in the plane of this meridian, its spinning-Axis will point its N end up to, and continue to point truly up to the Celestial pole. One first recognizes the fact that all rotating bodies-fly-wheels of steam engines and the link-are always tending to turn themselves towards the Polestar; gently and vainly tugging at their foundations, all the time they are in motion, to get round towards the object or adoration.*" [119]

Myrrha *Greek*, transformed into a myrrh tree when pregnant, and from this tree her child was delivered. We can find some myths as local beliefs and traditions in rural cultures too, where the tree splits itself open to deliver the child, and sometimes a hatchet opens the tree and frees the child, which is called a god or Divine Child, or in the case of an adult, we have a Divinity, such as Vishnu suddenly coming forth from a pillar as it bursts open as mentioned in the RigVeda.

Myths perpetuated as local beliefs and traditions in rural cultures too can be found such as where the spirit of a baby can be invited out of a tree by a woman wanting to bear children. Compare this to the Somatic Ritual that I wrote about in "Italian Magic: Secret Lives of Women" where rural women in Umbria would go to trees to take the spirits of their coming babies, specific sacred trees which have been and split open by lightning who have the magical elderberry growing out of the split, and Aboriginal Australians have a similar belief. And round the world are beliefs that both Tree Deities and Stone Deities create human beings from their earthly matter.

Artemis Orthia, Artemis Podagra, *Greek:* Artemis Orthia, was also called by the name *Lygodesma*, which means Willow-Bound because a wooden image of her was found in a willow. [120] Compare to *Artemis Podagra*: Artemis of the gout, whose etymological root: pod-**Ag**ra would actually mean White Footed, meaning *of celestial space, a foot-bound or fixed Axis* like Oidipous...[121] and whose **Ag** root word denotes "*one wh*o **agg**s *the Universe round*, brining us to the Black Magnetic Stone Mountain.

Terminus, *Roman*: The god Terminus, a very archaic god in the records, and whose name means *of the extremity*, a deeply rooted eternal Pillar, an unshakeable Axis god who withstood all the gigantic strain of the vast universe that turned upon him. God of the socket, the end, the pivot of that Axis. [122] Being a stone Deity, he was also venerated through stone Boundary stones, as I write about in rural Italian practice in "Italian Magic: Secret Lives of Women." When he was represented by a statue, there was a hole cut into any roof he was under or he was found in an entirely roofless archaic temple…and his image was a "*long, squared upright stone or a tree stump*" [123] and, as was often with supreme heavens Deities, represented as developed, with just a head on top of a Pillar, no arms, no legs, no body, representing his dwelling at the top end of the axis, versus the gnarled foot of a rooted tree divinity axis that has contact with the earth.

Asherah, *Syria, Palestine*: "**marriage of tree with ston**e" The *Asherah* is a tree post or pole with ornaments which formed the consecrated simulacrum of the Chthonian goddess of fecundity and life in the Canaanite worship of Palestine. [124] This means of course, there's a Deity venerated through this tree post, who is *Asherah*, also given the name *Baalat*, because as a Deity, while she was paired with *El*, she was also envisioned coupled with *Baal*. Baal is a Mountain Deity among other roles towards Divine Motion. Lat means Stone Pillar. *Asherah* also simply means "single tree pole" and was venerated through the pole as a Tree Goddess. *El* or *Eloha*, is a stone Deity, *Elohim* is the plural for meaning stone Deities, which makes *beth-Els*, the stone houses animated by Stone Deities.

So *Asherah*, or *Asherim* (plural) as connective objects to Cosmos space *was a figment of the Cosmic tree, which was also the Tree of life.* [125] In the myths of Asherah, she is also connected to water, given the generic term *water goddess*.

The true meaning of Water Deities is:
- As Creators who are part of the Moisture Principle
- As Deities of the Polar Zone who dwell and have Duty towards either the Black Stone Mountain; the area where the Heavens-River emanates, in the Celestial "waters" that is constant and stable; or as a star in the Universe-Ocean. *Water goddess* is a contemporary term that means nothing as related to Cosmic Space, which is what all the archaic practices who use *Asherim* as a symbol of Deity are based on.

This diagram is of a rural amulet called a cimartua; in short, cima di ruta, literally, means "top of the rue plant". It is decorated with medico-magical images of domestic mother-magic, and is similar to Asherim decorations in intention. This version is inverted, but all decorations of trees are on the tree TOPS, whose significance you'll find at the end of this chapter.

And, as a Deity associated with the Universe-Tree-Axis as a wooden pole or post, a stone pillar or column, as well as the Polar Zone of waters, there would be Blood Sacrifices (or their later simulacrum made of reeds or straw or other items resembling the Axis) required.

In the same category is the *Yupa* or sacrificial post which is hymned in the RigVeda as a typical tree or Lord of the Wood (Vanaspati) and is "well-clad and hung with wreaths," and which was a living tree or a tree-like post, planted in the ground like an English Maypole or a French *arbre de Liberte*. In Assyria also ornamental poles were planted beside portable altars. [126]

Volundr, *Norwegian:* of the Norse Edda loses the use of his feet which makes him fixed to a central axial position [127], meaning he is an Axis Deity, but he is involved in other functions that I'll mention in my next book.

AgLauros, *Greek*: a female Tree Divinity, connected to other Axis Deities male and female in her myths, such as PalLas and Hermes who are also Stone Deities whose name indicates the Tree, beam or Shaft on which the **Ag**ging of the Universe was supposed to be carried on, recalling that:
-Sanskri **aj**- -Avestan **az**--Greek **ayw**--Latin-**ago**-midIrish **ag**aim--oldNorse **aka**-
all have the same signification of *driving*…And *Laurus* being the baytree.[128]

Further, this cosmic root ***ag*** is the real origin of Greek **ay**iov in the sense of Sanctuary (or holy things) in Cosmic space, here in the Polar zone of which would be the inner-Heavens, the Arcana Treasures within the Heavens-Palace, the Stone Thrones and other powers and secrets of Immortal Deities.

In on of her myths, PalLas plays a role. Pal**Las** is a female Stone Deity of the **Pal**, or Spear, which is a specific Stone tool of the gods often used to "stake the earth" or, to mark a place for a new city or land-island (city on earth). Thus all Spear Deities are also Stone Deities and from Triads in the Celestial Polar Zone of the Black Magnetic Mountain.

Cybele was called: the Great PaLadin of Ida

PalLas turns **Ag**Lauros into a stone, after which means that the Tree-Axis Deity of **Ag**Lauros is now also a Stone Deity with specific powers of Birthing beginnings of sacred places that will be marked with Navel/Ompahlos stones. Therefore **Ag**Lauros is an Axis Stone-Pillar Deity. Just as with trees of different types, there are also Pillars of different types: Protection pillars, pillars marking Polar zones or representing a Deity, double pillars marking entry to the Gates of Heaven, and more. The World-pillar, like the World of Universe-Tree, is also a marker of Divinities who can touch down on earth…it's a sign of access as seen in myths where a stone pillar is in the middle of the ocean or sea, with only its base to be seen as the highest of its height disappears into the sky because it's so tall it's reaching to the Polestar.

When referring to the Deity who sits atop this Pillar , or whose consciousness is at the other end of it, "**Ag**Lauros is a mediating savior from the height of the **Ak**Ropolis". [129]

This diagram is of a Black Madonna inside a glass tube that has closures on both top and bottom, looking remarkably like a Axis, Pillar, or tube of transport. It is a sketch of an actual sculpture in St. Peter's Basilica in Oirschot featured on interfaithmary.net

Other trees whose function was tied to the Axis but also other aspects of the Cosmos:-**Y**g**g**drasil Ash *Old Norse* meaning "powerful whirler" its MOTION: **ag**ging, -IrminSul *Old Saxon*, -Haoma, *Zoroastrian, Persian* -Kalpavriksha *Buddhist, Hindu*

Whether Osiris or any of these other Divine Beings, the space around which their bodies are *engulfed by the earth or the tree trunks*, in these cases, *becomes the column which sustains the roof of a royal palace*, so it's a structure that is part of a turning mechanism ; imagine an Axis, with a pivot point at the Polestar, and then the Divine duty of holding up a part of celestial space in a larger sense, but also the Heavens-Palace where there is the Arcana of secrets and other Cosmic knowledge kept by the gods.

The Axis, as a Cosmic structure, is in fact Fixed into the Mountain by mechanism of a pivot. Though it rotates, it is non-dancing: it's attached to Moving parts: the rest of the Cosmos, all the dancing stars. The Pivot is connected to the base elements of the Mountain; the Universe-Tree-Axis is ultimately in service of the Black Stone Mountain and allows Ascended Masters to use it for travel. The Tree Branches serve another duty, the Tree Roots yet another.

===

HELIADES

Heliades, The Tree Sisters of which there are 7 and who have 7 brothers. This is a reference to Ursa Major and Ursa Minor, thus they are connected to the Polar region. It is common in worldwide myth to find 7 Helpers from the Ursas.

Here, specifically, the daughters, that is, the daughters of Elios, meaning of El a Great Central god and **not** of the sun…like beth-Els which were animated stone-houses of Deities. Elios was before Sun worship began just as Amaterasu of Japan was, who later had "sun goddess" tacked onto her name and myth. The Heliades are Universe-Tree dryad divinities because *they were turned into Poplar trees* in their myth.

There are several myths about the Heliades with widely different parents, some stories telling of only 3 sisters, which would indicate a TRIAD Deity, meaning that they still would be connected to the Polar zone in a traditional way, while Pleiades cannot be.

The list of Daughters with names that make most sense as a group, etymologically is: Merope, Helie, Aegle, Lampetia, Pheobe, Aetherie, Dioxippe…because they are Axis Deities, meaning, they have a connection to the Central Heavens and their names are connected to this Bright area of the Cosmos which is that has been examined here: the Polestar, Ursa Major and Ursa Minor, the Black Stone Mountain and its partnership with Trees, and the Axis that is anchored underneath the Black Magnet Mountain which spins the rest of the Cosmos.

The 7 brother Heliades all have etymological names related to that Black Magnetic Motion: **Ag**, **Ak**..and the like. As for the Daughters, their names explain their connection to the Polar Zone:
- *Merope* = face turned, One-eyed, the significance of will be related to the Polestar Deities
- *Helie* = of **EL**ias, remembering that a beth-EL is a stone house for a Deity, and that Elios written Helios) was a most archaic pre-sun worship Deity of this Supreme Central zone in the Cosmos.
- *Aegle* = Shining, Radian , as often the White Heavens are referred to
- *Lampetia* = Shining
- *Pheobe* = Bright, Shining
- *Aetherie* = Clear sky
- *Dioxippe* = Horse Driving (the importance of this will be revealed in my next book)

So the Heliades, in being turned to Trees, exactingly their bodies consumed by Tree Trunks and turning into Axis Divinities of the "Bright, Shining Heavens".

===

Madonna della Quercia
Tree Tops

The story I was told about *Madonna della Querica* in the Campania region of Italy was that during the war, when soldiers were creeping through farm fields, locals living there and caught out in their fields (one person at a time, these were various stories), only had an Oak tree to hide around. So they prayed to the Madonna of the Oak for protection, and said that soldiers would creep right by them, not noticing them at all, as if they were invisible.

In paintings of *Madonna della Querica* that I've copied in this chapter, you'll notice She or her Image is in the Tree Tops, not among the trunk, nor at the roots. The top of the tree has significant aspects to it within the Cosmic zone:
- literal fruits and leaves as food and medicine for humans, created first in Celestial space
- plant parts that are made into special drinks that alter consciousness and unlock Secrets of the Gods
- and Zodiacal fruit, in other words, Souls who can become Human Beings by taking a path through the

ecliptic as it intersects with the Galactic Center and who then enter a physical embodied life on earth: the 12 fruits of Universal Tree which are the 12 zodiac signs on the ecliptic, the 12 possibilities or paths for a soul to take on as a physically embodied human.

A tiny sampling of examples of the above:
- Irish Tree Tops offering Celestial nourishment, in very truncated parts of myth there is the Rowan tree of Celestial space where the divine De Danaans brought its berries from their Celestial Land of Promise so they'd have nourishment on their journey. But as they passed through an old Oak wood, one of the berries fell to Earth and from it grew an enormous, great tree which exhibited all the virtues and fruits of its Celestial counterpart.
- Chinese peaches have this same genesis in Celestial space and the same **magic**al properties
- Babylonian date-palms as the Tree of Life have the same reference.

Sacred Plants that offer alterations of the mind to access Divine secrets:

- The Egyptian *nefer* plant has its parallels in:
- the Avestan white *Haoma*,
- the *Soma* and *Fleur-de-Lis* and it also symbolizes the white crown of the Polar zone,
- the Norse *Balder*, the whitest of all plants, and all these and other sacred white plants were made into a sacred juice then placed into the *Graha* (small cup, *graal*) while ritualistically facing North of the Polar zone and placing the Graha on the top of a mound replicating the Mountain which is the higheest High place in all the Cosmos.

The Graha vessel or cup resembles a mortar in shape, and also has a small saucer of clay to put over the soma-vessel to cover the precious intoxicating soma-juice, the sacrificial wine of these archaic Indian sacrifices. Graha means also a cupful of the Soma. Graha primarily means to Seize, or the Seizer, to grasp, and the soma is also food, also the breath. [130]

Photos by Karyn Crisis from Trieste, Italy

This is what the Ephesus statue which bears several Goddess names actually is referring to: The Tree of Life. The legs are the Axis and its chest are are not breasts (show me a classical Greek or Roman statue that has breasts like that) but the seeds of the Fruits, here, like palm seeds that fell from

Celestial space to make physical trees on earth. The bees on the Axis are the stars that revolve and round the Mountain and its Axis…other animals refer to the Constellations of the Polar Zone, keeping in mind that for some cultures they are oxen or cow and in others they are bears. There is even a symbol for the 4 Cardinal directions within a Celestial sphere.

SUMMARY

The **Black Madonnas**, or the preceding Deities they replaced, have claimed, in their Duty towards Divine Motion, The Axis as one who revolves or turns round, and the Axis as a means of travel reserved for Ascended Masters, and as Tree Tops, as one who gives various forms of Life and Sustenance.

Egyptian and other Conical cap-wearers, whether in sacred plant medicine rituals or as priests of Deities, mimic the Mountain and all its sacred knowledge.

The **Black Madonnas** move through the Axis but dwell in the Heaven's-Palace of the Mountain atop the Axis where the secret knowledge is kept and can be accessed in part by sacred plants, but in part in Cosmic space, or energetically: as everything has its genesis in the Celestial first, and physical and energetic are components of everything and one is not without the other.

CHAPTER 5: PILLARS

"Madonna, Madonna
That you are the pillar of heaven
That you are the ladder of paradise,
Help those who call you,
Now that I call you
Help me in my need" [131]

Photo of the Heavenly Gates outside Chiesa di San Bernardino di Siena by Karyn Crisis

The Pillar Axis
Pillars as Protectors of Portals
Our Lady of the Pillar

The symbols connected with **Black Madonnas** in this book thus far come together in a mysterious place just 10 driving minutes outside of the city of Benevento in an area called *lo stretto di Barba*, the strait of Barba. Recalling a similarity: *"the main Deity of Assyria, Babylon, Syria and*

Phoenicia dwelt in the highest heaven, and also on Mountains, on the high places on earth; and was represented in preference by one of many columns, pyramids or obelisks in the temples before them. He was called El or Elio, the Most High: Bel or Ba'al the Master, and other epithets[...] Baal-Peor = Belphegor=lord of the opening, slit, or mountain pass." [132]

In the Strait of Barba are, notably: -Mountain pass or strait, -the Mountain, -the river, -the tree, -separation of heavens and earth, the **Black Madonna** (here called Mamma Schiavona), a Mountain peak temple-turned-church, Portals and Protectors, the physical manifestation of Deity...and the symbolic usage of Pillars which this chapter features.

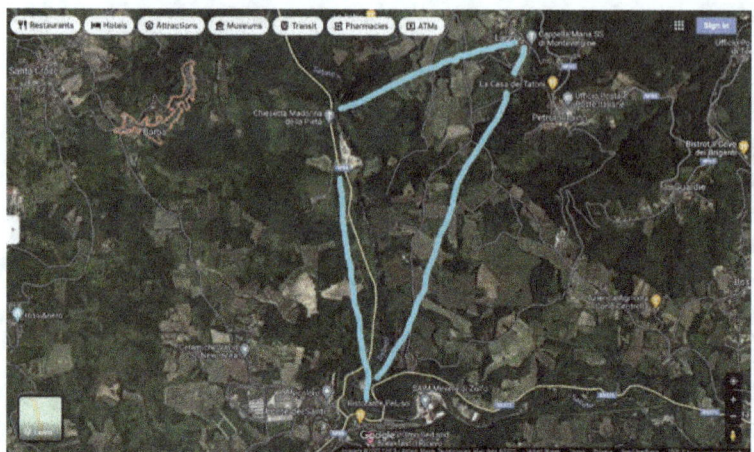

On Left, overview of the lo stretto di Barba and extended area from Google maps, on Right, Karyn with Carlo Napolitano and Jenny Capozzi in the strait of Barba showing one mountain cliff

The mysterious *bewitched triangle* of this area as Carlo Napolitano calls it, there is as he discovered, a triangular formation of churches. One of them, *Chiesetta Madonna della Pieta*, is constructed right against the road in an unusual way because there's no sidewalk walking space between the front of the church and the road, and it's also in the strait of Barba, a very narrow road that passes between 2 mountains..or what looks like one mountain cut in half, like the mythic Greek Cyanean/Kuanean [133] Black Clashing Rocks that allow or disallow passage in the Highest Astral realms to the Heaven's Palace and Black Mountain...or who prevent passage.

Overview of the Chiesetta Madonna della Pieta, from Google maps

CHAPTER 5: PILLARS

Chiesetta Madonna della Pieta is built in a particular way: one simple square room, flat facade with 4 flattened columns carved into it. Directly opposite it on the other side of the narrow street are 2 Trees that look like 2 columns, mimicking the columns of the church facade. Interestingly for the symbolism of the Black Mountain, there is a church with the same facade structure at Montevergine called *Torrione* the Tower. They look nothing like towers. See the next chapter for more.

Though a narrow paved road has been made between the trees and church, and on the other side of the trees are railroad tracks, this tight arrangement has been preserved and has been paved around. Behind *Chiesetta Madonna della Pieta* is dense forest, and further into the land are alleged ancient remnants of other structures. There is also a legend attached to the Mountain peaks here, that a woman jumped to her death from one of them. Likely this is a symbolic myth, meant to help us remember that a Divine Woman jumped i.e. traveled through the High Black Magnetic Mountain down to earth, the *Chiesetta Madonna della Pieta* to physically manifest…**and she would have had to do so via the Axis, as a Pillar**.

Left, photo of Chiesetta Madonna della Pieta by Karyn Crisis, and photo of the Trees in front of it.

At the 3rd church, which has been built next to an olive tree, perhaps there was once a well, or the tree came first: *Chiesa di San Bernardino di Siena.*This is a strange name insertion, in an area of the Divine Feminine, for all the hatred San Bernardino had towards esoterica, women, spirituality…he was known for his damning speeches that incited hatred of "the other." In Chianchetelle, a village to the east of the Sabato River is *Chiesa di Santa Margherita,* where there is a a man-made construction that you see in the opening small photo of this book: 2 pillars that have tops that look like trees, and the Virgin Mary in the middle…notice the vines as well. This structure, like the actual church, is marking the heavens on earth, and the constructed version lets you know you're near the church itself, the place that's the Portal, the Door to the Celestial double.

The 2nd church, *Cappella Maria SS di Montevergine,* whose front door and site above the door points to *Santuario di Montevergine* and its **Black Madonna** painting and pilgrimages, features a miniature copy of the Mamma Schiavona painting, which I discuss in the next chapter.

Out of all 3 churches, *Chiesetta Madonna della Pieta* is the only one built on the 4 Cardinal Points

axis: its door opens on the East (Rebirth) side and so, facing the altar, you would be looking West (death). To exit, one would be reborn again moving to the East direction. The other 2 churches are built on diagonals.

Pieta is also the church that the locals hold in fear and awe, as they believe it's highly haunted and protected by spirits, which is something Napolitano writes about at length in his book "*il triangolo stregato, il istero del noce di Benevento*". He shares local and personal stories about the spirits preventing people from coming here, sometimes in the form of an Old Man and Old Woman, which could be spirits of the Mountain, as Original Creator Deities were known by these names. He also told me the Goddess had touched down on earth here, and I don't think he knew, at that time, how correct he was. I also mention one of my experiences with the electric energy of the Divine here as well as what it felt like to sense the hundreds of protecting spirits in my first book "Italy's Witches and Medicine Women Vol 1." My 3rd visit here, I also experienced 2 enormous Beings-in-spirit, like twins, who were not only protecting the site but were also teaching me, and have continued to teach me. This is interesting because years later I've discovered that as related to **Black Madonnas** and the beliefs within this book, Portals are protected by twins: dual pillars as dual Deities, or as twin constellations like Castor and Pollux.

The AXIS, in general

The envisioned AXIS has been a way for oral peoples to account for Deities traveling from the Cosmic skies, down to the earth, and back up again, which is something reserved for Ascended Masters, because it is not simply a way that Beings-in-spirit travel from their realm to the earth realm: this instead is for Beings who have ascended to a High realm but have not decided to merge with Source again and instead retain their Identity as a Helper or Teacher, and who take the physical body they last used on earth up to Cosmic space with them (by turning it into light) and can come back down to earth to re-inhabit it. This means they do not take the usual soul process of moving through the zodiac ecliptic and into a human fetus body where they will have to grow again, forgetting who they are as a soul and all their soul experiences, attempting to remember their Divinity throughout their human life.

An example, keeping in mind that a *fairy king* would be classified as a Celestial Deity:
"*A Russian fairy-king hides his children in or upon a pillar to remove them from the attacks of a devouring Bear whose fur is of iron*". [134] This tale is speaking about the Axis as a means of hiding in its technical aspect of travel, as inside an elevator, for example, and the Bear of iron is speaking of the Ursa Major and Ursa Minor constellations that revolve round the Black **Mag**netic Mountain and never leave from there...this mythic template about Iron being drawn to the Black Mountain is explored more deeply in my next book. There are so many myths about Loadstones referring to this.

There are different versions of the Axis envisioned, because there are believed to be different types of Deities who are in charge of different parts of Divine Cosmic Motion. So Axis is a general mechanical term, and different types of Axis are, for example: Pillars, tall standing stones, Poles, Posts and Columns, Trunks (of wood), Boats, Round Towers, Obelisks, Minarets, the Spear, Vines and Reeds. Some Deities are travelers, as mentioned above, while other Axis Deities are responsible for keeping the cosmos moving or dancing round it, as it takes everything along with it *to the right*, in service of the Black Stone Mountain which causes this rotation, this gyration, with its **mag**netism.

Just as with a Mill grinder (that the Axis has also been envisioned as) having different mechanical parts all working together, with each part having a specific individual motion and also a relationship to the Motion of the whole: the literal **ax**le, the post, the stone grinder that moves around the post, the bottom stone area that is unmoving, and all the other smaller parts. It has been envisioned that

Deities have also individually specific parts of the Axis that they govern and areas they have access to in their duties towards Divine Motion and their various allowances of access of the Cosmos.

Accordingly, some Deities are associated with for example, the Tree Roots while others are associated with the Tree Tops (Ephesus statue) and others the Tree Trunk. It is the same with the Pillar tops, the pillar base, the lateral sides of the pillar, etc. In one example, the Axis, in its part towards keeping Divine Motion, is pivoted into the Black Stone Magnetic Mountain, but also envisioned as a stable item that revolves and has the Cosmos move round it; connected but also separate.

Pillars as Axis of Connection

PILLARS also represent a connection between the Heavens and Earth, which is needed because of a belief that the Heavens and Earth separated long ago, thus separating the earth from Celestial structures and its Deities. The Milky Way hemispheres are envisioned as a representation of this: the Northern Hemisphere is masculine and also west; the Southern Hemisphere is feminine and also east.

On the lower left, of the Left image, imagine that as a man, a pied piper shape, if you will. On the lower Right, a woman sitting with pregnant belly: this is where the Galactic Center is. Horizontally, this is the way these arms of the Milky Way wrap around the 4 Cardinal Directions. So, comparing the 2, you can see that based on how the Milky Way appears to change in the sky (horizontal v vertical), the South becomes East, the North becomes West.

The pillar, or Axis, would extend through the 4 Cardinal Directions in Celestial space down through the earth and past its globe, into the Mountain that's at the South Celestial pole.

Pillars that support the Center of a dwelling, like the Center beam of a Celestial House and serves as a means of travel back and forth from Heavens to Earth, to the vital stations of the Polar Mountain zone, such as the Palace, Treasury, Arcana, and Tree Fruits: This device appears in myths about the Heavens-Palace which is supported by the Pillar. Here is an example from the equatorial rain forests of the Columbian Northwest Amazon: *"The Malocas, or longhouses, of the Tukano are built to be miniature models of the universe. They are always built with their main axis pointing east/ west, the direction of rivers and the Sun's passage across the sky. Three pairs of large forked posts and their respective beams separate the interior space of the Maloca. The sections are joined together from above by a single beam. This central beam is said to symbolize the Milky Way, which connects the three worlds and lies on the east-west axis. Interestingly, the word for the beam is gumu. The words gumu and kumu come from the same origin and mean "axis". Kumu is the title used to describe the most powerful shaman in the tribe. Gumu can also refer to a bridge created from a single trunk. Again, we see a ladder symbolizing the connection between Earth and the Otherworld, the Milky Way.* [135]

For examples of Jack and the Beanstalk as an Axis of connection, see Chapter 7.

Photo by Eline Kinsenbergen of Our Lady of the Oak. She holds a spear, reminding us that she is an Axis Deity with the ability to move up and down the Axis, and the glass tube around her is another reminder of this, imagine an elevator of sorts, accessible for Ascended Masters.
Used with permission. https://www.facebook.com/eline.kinsbergen.9 ; from interfaithmary.net

Pillar As Creator Duo Deity,
As Individual Deity

There are Pillars that were venerated as Animated Stones, that is, embodying some of the Spirit of specific Deities. These were not carved into human shapes but rather represented, numerically, with the 4 Cardinal directions as a 4-sided pillar, or the 1/2 cardinal directions as an 8-sided pillar or even 16-sided. Other pillars were simply round, in the case of Axis Deities who also were considered to be Mountain Deities: in these cases, the pillar might also have a conical cap on top, representing the Mountain. Later in time, some pillars would display just the Head of its Deity: no arms nor legs nor feet nor torso.

Photos of a Pillar Column at a castle in Leonessa, Rieti, Italy, which shows the faces of the 4 Cardinal directions (one has been hammered off).

A few examples of Deity and Pillars:

- from the Congo: *"Inside there was a circular mound of worked clay with patterns traced in the clay by means of coloured beads and pebbles. On opposite sides of the mount stood 2 figures, unmistakably male and female, about 4 feet high, and on stakes passing up through the roof were spitted outside some European plates and dishes, the stakes passing through the holes made in their centres. Here we have clearly vestiges of the mythical mountain, of dual primeval Deities."* [136]

- *"In China, on the road from Na-chi Hsien , square pillars of stone, with the carved head of of Amita Buddha at their tops. At a distance they look just like Roman terminal statues and are loaded with votive offerings. Amita the Immeasurable is chief of all Buddhas, here represented as a Northern supernal Deity at the point of the earth-Axis."* [137]

- In more symbolic, subdued form Pillars are found, singular and as doubles, in scenes on Etruscan mirrors.

- Obelisks were adored in this same way, as embodying Deity

- *"El, the Semitic god-name, has for its primitive sense 'a column.'"* [138]

By Karyn Crisis, photo of the Obelisk from the Temple of Iside in the city of Benevento, Campania

Because the Axis, the Mountain and all its parts are envisioned as being mechanical as well as alive with Deities who care for its Motion, there is of course a connection between the column, the cone (or Pivot and Mountain top) and the Mountain: the column being the Axis which not only leads to these places but is pivoted into the Mountain and assists with moving the entire cosmos 'round it. And, that these places and their zones are inhabit by the Deities who have Duties towards them. These Pillars also demanded blood sacrifice, and over time, substitutions using natural items that represent these mechanical parts.

"The Pillar, as a visible embodiment of Deity,
in the process of time came to be fashioned into a statue of stone,
as the sacred tree or post developed into an image of wood,
and on a more direct line, [..] into the tower,
the minaret, the steeple,"[139]
and all in service to the Black Magnetic Mountain.

Pillars
as Protectors of Portals

Pillars, usually used in a pair, serve as Guardians to Portals in both Celestial Spaces and terrestrial spaces, such as the Pillars to the Gate of Heaven. This is what exists at *Chiesetta Madonna della Pieta.* As to their power to reach from the Celestial realms into the earthly realms, I'd recommend reading Napolitano's book about how people are prevented from coming here, if the Spirits deem them not welcome. Some stories are quite frightening. Or, if you visit the area and get to know the locals, you can ask their opinions and see the emotions on their faces. Some people won't even even want to talk about it.

Chapter 9 discusses why this area is so important, the next Chapter does as well. It's a very loaded place. And, as you can see in the Google overview image, the Triangular shape the churches take is none other than the symbol for the Tree of Life, which points to the actual Portal for the **Black Madonna's** pillared passage down to earth and back up again.

Pillars are often seen in front of tombs, entryways, in front of portals to Celestial spaces that contain knowledge and the securest treasures of the universe. They always represent Deities or Protectors of these Passageways. The Greek Clashing Rocks are just one other stone version of Protectors of these Passageways.

If you've read "Italian Magic: Secret Lives of Women," I wrote about the seriousness with which border stones are taken in rural Italy, to the point where people often cannot release into death due to the guilt they may have if they secretly moved a border stone of their neighbor (under passages about *s'Accabbadora*). Border stones have been revered and considered with sanctity, and it's not surprising then that a Roman god is named Terminus who not only has to do with the Pillar-Axis, but also borders and boundaries. As border stones are stones, they are believed to have the spirit of Deities alive within them.

Our Lady of the Pillar of Zaragoza, Spain is seen in various depictions: always a Black carved statue on a pillar. Sometimes this pillar looks triangular like a Mountain, and at other times there are gold halos behind her, leaving a triangular Mountain-like shape behind her.

===

Our Lady of the Pillar

The legend of Our Lady of the Pillar of Zaragoza, in the region of **Ar**agon in northeastern Spain, is *one of the oldest Marian invocations* which generally claims:

-Allegedly, St James, named one of the *sons of thunder* (1) by Jesus,
was trying to bring the gospel of Jesus to Spain in 40 A.D.
-He was struggling in this endeavor and in a moment of need,
he knelt down at a river's edge. (2)
-Suddenly he heard singing of angels, (3)
and claims he saw the Virgin Mary, not just a vision of her, but that she
bilocated while allegedly living physically embodied in Ephesus at this time. (4)
She was standing on top of a six foot pillar, in his experience. (5)
-The Virgin Mary asked him to build a church here
and have it consecrated to her, (6)
and requested he incorporate the Pillar and the statue of herself holding baby Jesus. (7)

The components of this story are common symbols regarding Pillar Deities and used to remind us of their Cosmic zone:
1. Connection to Thunder, Black Stone Mountain, Pillar and Axis
2. The Challenge
3. Initiation through music, song
4. Divine Intervention
5. The Axis symbol, Pillar as Deity
6. Marking heavens on earth, as an Omphalos
7. Remembrance, a symbol that points to Cosmic origin and meaning

1. St James and Thunder. The fall of aerolites, our Black iron-infused magnetic stones, have long been venerated as being Divine, from the Black Stone Mountain of the Polestar, and even in their raw form venerated as Deities. As aerolites, they are *"generally accompanied by the visible luminousness of the meteor and an explosion," which was often confounded with thunder* [140] and became a popular belief that the thunderbolt is a stone, or associated with these stones. It is common to find this belief among oral peoples worldwide. As such, these stones were venerated, kept in the pockets as amulets, used in protection medicine bags, and more. Further, the Sacred Mountain, in Japan, for example, is associated with elements and "thunder gods" such as Kagu-tsuchi [141] having a name whose etymology of "chi" termination in names used with gods having to do with thunder, and matches Norse beliefs about thunder as well as we find in the myth of the god Perun who is a Thunder and Mountain Deity, and many other examples that can be named. So the connection between Black Stone Mountain, the Black magnetic stones there, the central cosmic north and thunder originates here, not with the christian story.
2. The river, in these myths, always refers to the Heavens-River aka the Milky Way, alluding to Cosmic space.
3. The angels initiated people with song as well as humans who initiated people through song and dance.
4. Divine Intervention is a part of all Mythic Templates, and here the Virgin Mary offers hers by way of the Pillar-Axis that she is Deity of.
5. The Axis is her symbol, thus her statue is found at the top of it, since it's where she dwells in Cosmic space.
6. Axis Deities, armed with spears, use them to mark the Heavens on Earth by designating places that sacred sites should be the center of.
7. Wooden Image. Our Lady of the Pillar is carved of wood, reminding us of the Universe-Tree-Axis.

And, in accordance with this being the oldest Marian invocation, it's lovely to read that *"the Spanish consider that the pillar is a symbol of the duct connecting heaven and earth* [142] along with the belief that *Mary is the gate of heaven* because these are traces of archaic beliefs that existed long before the Christian canon was written. [143]

Somatic Ritual: In keeping with these beliefs, there is also appropriately a Procession, a 9 day feast with flowers and fruits (no doubt of the Tree Top of Life that she represents) to *Neustra Señora del Pilar* with music and dancing, which is one of the archaic ways of keeping inner secret knowledge alive. There is also a parade of Giants, which is significant for the Central Heavens Cosmic zone which I'll elaborate on in my next book. This Procession and celebration takes place in October.

SUMMARY:

Black Madonnas, or the previous Deities they have replaced, have been portrayed as being Pillar Deities, specific Deities who have access to a means of travel as Ascended Masters, that is, coming back to earth with same physical body they left it with, rather than starting all over again as a soul being born into a physical body and then trying to remember its experiences until that point in all its various physical lives.

As a Pillar Deity, a **Black Madonna** (or multiples) would have a defined personality, rather than a soul that has Ascended and blended back with Source.

As a Pillar Deity, **Black Madonnas** would also enjoy the protection of other Deities, Constellation consciousness and other Beings as Protectors, symbolized by Dual Pillars.The Pillar is an inseparable mechanism of the Black Stone Magnetic Mountain.

CHAPTER 6: MOUNTAIN

MOUNTAIN

Let's go to the Mountain,
There is Mary who accompanies us:
She accompanies us this morning,
To collect the Dew.
The Dew is a sponge,
Bless our thoughts;
The Dew is in the Mint
Bless our Feelings:
The Dew is in the violets,
Bless the words;
The Dew is in the apples,
Bless our person,
The Dew is in the thyme,
Bless us, Beautiful Mother;
There is Lucifer who tempts us,
Bless the Holy Mother [144]

====

All across the world there can be found Mythical Mountains such as:

- India's Divine **Mount Meru** of the Cosmic center which has an earthly counterpart: Meru Peak in a mountain of the Himalayas in the state of Uttarakhand, India.

- The Celestial **Mount Ida** of the Polar center zone has a terrestrial counterpart in Phrygia (associated with the goddess Cybele) as well as in Crete (associated with Rhea). These are 2 separate mountains and 2 entirely different Mother Goddesses.

- Japan's cosmic and divine metal mountain, **Mount Kagu**, has its terrestrial counterpart as one of the 3 Yamato Mountains. Both Kagu and Yamato have etymological roots taking them to this central cosmic zone. Archaic somatic ritual dances performed here which are connected with primeval polar worship, as is the number 3. [145]

- **Mount Kasios** / Casius near the mouth of the Orontes River on the Syrian-Turkish border where a Black Stone god was venerated in its natural, aerolite (meteorite fallen from the heavens) form and as a conical (mountain-shaped) stone.

- **Chicomoztoc**, the 7-caved Divine Universe-Mountain of Mexico also called Teo-Culhuacan the lofty arched mountain of the gods, is situated in a lagoon (the figurative Universe-ocean) in Aztlan, which means whiteness, here, *"Whiteness of the Heavens."*[146] This is a parallel idea to the Egyptian White Wall, the Bright Firmament of the heavens, and all the other *whiteness* references to this highest celestial zone.

- Irish **Hill of Tara**, was called Meath- or Mid-court, Miodhchuarta, all meaning: middle of, central, reminding us of the Mountain in the Central Heavens, 'round which the universe revolves, and which is also an Omphalos. Earthly hills designated to this reminder represent these Celestial places with their etymology of names using the root meaning mid, central. The Tara hill myth (here very truncated) reinforces these ideas for remembrance: In Lochlann in the North (just as the Black Stone Mountain is in the Celestial North) is the hill of Miodhchaoin (or Midkena), jealously guarded by Miodhchaoinn and his 3 sons [147] : North, hills with names referencing Middle of heavens, a Protector whose name references the Central Heavens, and 3 sons = a Divine Triad. Cybele is also part of a Divine Triad, and Divine Triads dwell in the Polar North.

- Meath itself where this **Kilair** navel stood, was anciently the central one of the 5 divisions of Ireland, and is called **Med**ia […] and it would thus be the Middle-Kingdom. [148] These Central Heavens ideas also correspond to Chinese ideas of Central Heavens.

What's interesting about these Mountains, and the same goes for underworld caves and entrances, is that while places are marked on this earth with these names, the myths about them are referring to Celestial mountains in the sky and the Celestial underworld in the sky. None of the myths are historical accounts about happenings on planet earth. That's why myths, along with local legends, continue to hold an element of "unsolved mystery" and are haunting…because if you are looking for them on earth, you won't find them…but there are non-physical conscious beings and stars-as-matter/ energy and celestial locales that DO exist and are connected to these beliefs, and so their presences can be felt, like a ghost.

===

All across the world there can be found Myths about these Mountains such as:

- **Quaciou**, one of the chief gods of the Aramean peoples was an **aerolite** god [149], that is, a Deity of fallen meteorites, iron-infused **Black stones** from the Black Magnetic Mountain of the Polar Center of the Cosmos. He was adored in many places as a **mountain**-god. [150] [The earthly] Mount Kasios/ Mount Casius near Antioch was one of the seats [his **stone throne**] of Quaciou, and was regarded by the people as the god himself. At Selucia in Syria he was a heavens-fallen **conical stone** [151]. Conical stones, conical hats and headdresses were all representations of Celestial Mountain Deities, taking the shape of the space where the **Universe-Tree-Axis** pushes up into the Polar Zone and supports it. Thus, many Mountain Deities are also Axis gods…but there are different mechanical parts to the Axis as well, so there are different categories of Deities based on which aspect of Divine Motion they are responsible for and thus which part of the Axis they use such as the pivot of the Axis and the cave it creates, or the Heavens-Vault, or the Branches of the tree and the special items that grow there and how they are used and what wisdom they impart. Quaciou was also confused with Zeus Keraunios because so many Deities were venerated via **Black conical stones**, both masculine Deities and feminine.

- **Akrisios** is a **mountain**-top god of the supremest summit, the king of **Ar**gos.[152] (note here the **Ak** and **Ar** prefix and their etymological ties to the **Black Stone Mountain** at the center of the Cosmos round which the Universe turns), the **Universe-Axis**, and the power *to drive, to urge*. He is also simply the brilliant starry heavens. **Ak**risos was also a stone god, having been turned into a stone.

- **Cittaliene**/Citlalinicue: The Goddess and mother of Quetzalcoatl (with father Citlalatonac they are a Triad). She brought forth a flint dagger *tecpatl* that so alarmed her other sons that they flung the stone down from the height of heaven. It fell upon Chicomoztoc, the **7 caved divine universe-mountain**, and gave life to 600 gods and goddesses, of whom the principal were Quetzalcoatl and Tezcatlipoca [154]. Stories of Deities and humans coming from stones are found round the world. The reason Chicimoztoc (*chicome*, 7; *ostotl*, cave) [155] is called "7 Caves" because in the caves dwell the 7 tribes of the 7 sons of the lord of the Chicimoztoc paradise. This is connected to the Polar 7, the Ursa Major and Minor constellations.

- **Mount Kagu** has its origin in Celestial space's central Polar zone, and it's said to have descended its counterpart from heaven down to earth. Important parts of the myth are the *Kami* who live here at the base of the **tree trunks** on this **mountain**. *Kami* are an Original Creator Deities duo. This indicates the *Kami* are not only Polar Deities, but also Axis Deities connected with the Roots of the Axis. Further, this **mountain**, (as ALL celestial mountains of this specific nature and their counterparts on earth) have a special **rock cave** where specific divinities live and where certain knowledge is housed. This is a worldwide belief about caves.

Regarding blood sacrifices and their substitutions,
which are made to all Polar Deities and on High Places:
a simulacrum of human sacrifice, that is, a replacement for blood sacrifice utilizing symbols connected to Polar Zone sacrifice can be found in the somatic ritual performed for Mount Kagu. *There is an Archaic Shinto somatic ritual "Kagura dances" performed by girls at a famous temple in Nara.*
- They wear a white inner garment,
- loose red drawers,

- and a long gauzy mantle ornamented with the **Kasuga** crest of the Wistaria flower.
- A chaplet of artificial Wistaria and single scarlet camellia flowers crowns the forehead.
- Their faces are thickly painted white.
- They dance [...] to the accompaniment of a 3-priests-orchestra who perform drum and flute.[155] Wistaria/Wisteria is a Climbing Vine, which represents the Axis as a Connection between the Heavens and Earth.

All these symbols relate to the Polar North Zone, the red being of Blood Sacrifices, the 3 priests replicating a Triad Deity, and music an essential part expressing the Harmony of the Heavens and additional Cosmic knowledge, encoded. Note that Drums and especially the Flute are musical instruments associated with Cybele's somatic rituals as well, the Flute being an Axis symbol and used in hymns to the Axis Deities.

Mount Meru: **Mer** etymology: Merus = central, essential, also means Middle or Central Heavens, which is the Celestial Polar zone. This Hindu Mountain, the Celestial one, is where the Polar Deities dwell, and as all Celestial mountains, it is also part of the **Column/Axis/Pillar/Tree Trunk** Structure that once bridged the Heavens and Earth. As it is Centrally located, the **4 cardinal points** emanate from under it. On earth, it's a parallel of these highest celestial heights. On the **summit** of Mt. Meru, lives Indra with his female **dual principle** Indrani, and on the same golden mountain, as Kailasa, is the god Siva; for *Su-Meru, Maha-Meru, Kailasa, Kala-ya, and Suralaya* are all to be taken as one and the same heavenly peak; and all these names can be applied equally well to the Himalaya, which to the geographer becomes a mere terrestrial **mountain** chain. [156]

The foundational idea of the Mountain is that it's the Center from which everything is created as well as the Source of all waters, thus a Cosmic Navel also, an Omphalos, and a sanctuary, place of neutrality in judgement (the 12 judges in 12 black caps), Stillness, and Power round which the Universe moves in the same direction perpetually. It's the Highest of the High places, and Highest of the High Deities were worshipped on mountains and sacrificed to. It's also the site of Cosmic Battles...

This is why in every culture where there was placed a stone in the earth called a navel or an omphalos: it was deemed to be the Center of the Earth and its purpose was also to point out stability, a place of natural judgement, which is why oracles sat next to the stones as well. These designated places were marked by Creator Deities with Spears.

Common in places like Italy, towns are built out from a central point. *Centro* means central part of the town. In the *centro* typically is a church, (likely originally a temple, since the city or town was a Cosmic version of the heavens and thus temples were built at a site where there was also a tree and or a water source, to mimic this Great Celestial Mountain). Or, in the case of Mountains, pilgrimages were made there to the temple or later, to a church, if a town was not in fact built around it and because Mountain Tops were places of veneration for the Highest of the High Deities. Round towers were also built for a similar function, although often built instead of a guide-post for the living people to come to this Celestial place on earth, Round Towers, representing the Universe-Tree-Axis with windows aligned to the 4 Cardinal points, were built next to graveyards, so the dead could follow them upwards into the Milky Way, as Towers represent a Celestial structure.

===

All across the world mountain tops were set upon by altars,
properly aligned with the cardinal directions, utilizing these highest points on earth to emulate the Black Stone Mountain and its Polestar, those Supremely Highest-of-High locales and Highest Deity dwellings in celestial space: the stone altars bring Heavens down to earth.

The temples built around the altars, whether roofless and open-air or roofed, were specifically tailored and built to the type of Deity being venerated at the altar and which part of the Cosmic zone they represented examples: Black stones set into the earth as a singular Deity or as depicting the Zodiacal 12, singular pillars as Deity representations or in numerical symbolism depicting Protectors and Cardinal Directions, Cosmic treasures, paths, etc.

For example:

- **Quaciou**, one of the chief gods of the Aramean peoples, had made to him an open-air altar without a temple on the summit of Mount Kasios. He was also worshipped on another Mount Casius/Kasios at Pelusium (frontiers of Egypt and Palestine) where his idol was a young man holding a **pomegranate**.[157] The Greeks turned him into Zeus Kasios, but these were different and separate Deities.

- the god **Rimmon** was also envisioned with a **pomegranate**. Rimmon is a Syrian Deity considered a god of storm, rain and thunder, which makes him a Polar Deity as well as a Mountain Deity and a Black Stone (aerolite) Deity because of the Thunder connection. [158]
  The Hebrew word *rimmon* means pomegranate.

- **Cybele** also had temples built to her on mountain summits, and both she and **Attis** have been envisioned with a **pomegranate.** Cybele was just one of many Deities venerated as a black magnetic meteorite that fell from the heavens and was thus named, and that all Black Stone Deities are Central Heavens Deities with specific duties related to Divine Motion of the Polar Zone, specifically the Stationary, Compeller, Mountain and Cave presence of Stillness along with being Original Creator Duos of a Triad Divinity.

- A temple of **Ares** was set up as an open-air, roofless temple made of small stones. Inside a Black rock was fixed in the ground, and prayed to as it was sacred. Animal sacrifices were made to the altar of Ares which was outside the temple. [159]

- A **Mexican** myth tells of a shower of stones which fell from heaven, and among them a large rounded one named *techcatl* [160] in the form of a block which became the altar of human sacrifice. Showers of stones from heaven are common in every culture: sometimes they form islands, sometimes they form humans, and sometimes they are pieces of the Black Stone Mountain which contain spirits of Deities. In every culture there are myths about Deities throwing stones down to earth from Heaven. Stones were thrown to create specific types of physical matter on earth.

- **Perun**. In Belgium: not an altar, but a judgement seat, a place where oaths were taken, on a created structure that is elevated (recalling the 12 judges who reside in the Black Stone Mountain who wear Black conical caps). Here is a pillar on a 4-sided set of 3 steps [161]
  (nods to the cardinal points, Triad divinity, and a note that many of the sacred celestial ritual dances were 3-step dances). At its top is a fir cone (fruit of the Universe-Tree Branches at the top of the Axis) called a Peron, a Pillar. *Peron means stone.* [162]

- *Peron* as *Perun*, also a Deity of Slovenia, a god of Thunder (of which sound and atmosphere accompanies aerolite stones, that is, Black stones that fall from heaven)

- **AgLauros** depicted acting as a mediating Saviour on the supreme cosmic lofty rocks North of the **Ak**Ropolis called *Makrai Petrai*. This means they were centrally located as the Black Magnetic Stone, stable, neutral in judgement.[163] This calls to mind the **Black Madonna**, Mamma Schiavona of Cybele's Mountain in Partenio, of which myth there is a Divinity Savior on a lofty rock / Mountain peak.

This all comes together at MONTEVERGINE:

MONTEVERGINE
Originally the site of a temple of Cybele
who is known as Mountain Mother,
at the Highest of the High places on earth,
in parallel of Highest of the High zone in the Universe,
She is Creator of the Cosmos
and The Great **Pal**atina of Ida (which means stone spear)
And has been turned into the Black Madonna,
also named Mamma Schiavona.
Archaic Polar Deity worship dictates that her site of veneration be
somatically remembered with a Pilgrimage involving
Dancing + Singing,
and at this site are other symbols pointing to the Celestial Polar North:
A Tower hidden in plain sight,
A Zodiacal cosmic wooden throne
a Mythic Template of Resurrection..
and more…

Photo of Mt Partenio next to view looking down from Partentio, Montevergine. Photos by Karyn Crisis

Image number DDC249907
Accession Number: 1993.233
Title: Plaque of the Goddess Cybele
Date: 2nd-3rd century CE
Medium/Support: Leaded Bronze
Dimensions 10.3 x 9.3 x 1.2 cm (4 1/16 x 11/16 x 1/2 in.)
Credit Line: Harvard Art Museums/Arthur M. Sackler Museum, Gift of Max Falk in honor of Professor
David Gordon Mitten
photo Credit: Copyright President and Fellows of Harvard College
Persistent Link: https://hvrd.art/o/303850
Citation: *Plaque of the Goddess Cybele,* Harvard Art Museums/Arthur M. Sackler Museum, Gift
of Max Falk in honor of Professor David Gordon Mitten, Photo Copyright President and Fellows of
Harvard College, 199.233

Montevergine is:
- also called by the names *Partenio* and *Monti di Avella*.

- It's a mountain at 1,270 meters, just under the peak which is at 1,480 meters above sea level. It's located near Avellino in the commune of Mercogliano in the region of Campania.

- *It is pointed to* by a one-room church that is in the *triangolo stregato* as Carlo Napolitano calls this mysterious area of the *Stretto di Barba* where 3 tiny churches form a triangle. While all 3 are situated in strange ways, such as right up against the road, the *Cappella Maria SS di Montevergine* in particular is not aligned with the 4 Cardinal directions of NSEW grid as we'd imagine a church to be augured to. This is the chapel that *points to* Montevergine and it even exhibits a very sun-faded miniature version of the enthroned Mamma Schiavona painting on its exterior under a window that also acts as a sight rangefinder. (see images below by Karyn Crisis)

- It is the site of an ancient temple to Cybele. The Sanctuary of Montevergine was consecrated here in 1124, when the temple of Cybele was already in ruins.

- It now has a basilica in the complex of structures and here is where the painted-on-**wood** icon is located, the **Madonna nera**, known also as Mamma Schiavona. Its date is from sometime in the 13th century, Byzantine style. Originally it was just a painted head, and this head was added to the larger painting, including a **throne** and the Divine Child (which is truly zodiacal globally and not reserved for the infant jesus.). It has been placed between 2 **pillars,** and on the added frame is a hand-painted set of words: *nigraetform* (Latin for *Black form*) and *osaeamicamea* (Latin for *my female beloved*), and is supported by **8** angels

110

This painting, a smaller version of the one at the Santuario di Montevergine is inside the *Maria SS di Montevergine* that points to the Mountain Peak of the ancient Cybele temple. The actual painting is rather large and is fitted in-between 2 pillars and a split pointed roof as in the sketch. Photo by Karyn Crisis

- This complex also features also an octagonal* Abbey, important to note because this is not a random numerical choice. Ancient temple structures used 4 or 8 and even 16 to represent the cardinal or half-cardinal points in their structures of *heavens marking the earth*. Additionally, in temples and devotional monuments to Polar Deities who dwell in the Black Mountain, the cardinal points always factor in. Further, this numerical structure is used with Pillars, Columns and other structures built to represent the Universe-AXIS. And yes, the church, especially the Catholics, knew all of these things as a result of diligent efforts to catalog these beliefs. The number 8 often was used to refer to the entire Heavens, the holy of Holies. These 8 were also referred to as *8 unbounded gods* who live at the top of the Pillars, Column and Axis. 8 is used so often in the photos I've taken inside Italian churches and chapels.The half-cardinal points numerically represented by 8 can be seen in the opening full page photo of the Old Basilica in the circular ceiling design.

- An annual Pilgrimage is made here with remnants of ancient somatic ritual (song and dance) called *juta dei femminielli*.

- There's an old statue of a boy holding a pomegranate in the art museum of this complex that's on this mountain, and the pomegranate is a key symbol connected with other Divine Masculine children who became gods or who are Creator Deities of the Black Stone mountain like *Attis*, *Gibil*, *Baal* and *Rimmon*, and so there's also been created a **Madonna of the Pomegrante who** is depicted giving a pomegranate to baby jesus.

- It features some strategically placed trees: a large oak in front the Sanctuary complex, and 2 trees in front of the "Tower" which is a chapel, looking exactly like the one room churches/chapels in *Stretto di Barba*, but curiously here called *Cappella del Torrione*, and another large fenced-in oak in front of the Sanctuary.

"Torrione" photo by Karyn Crisis

L-R: *Cappella del Torrione,Chiesa di San Bernardino di Siena, Chiesetta Madonna della Pieta, Cappella Maria SS di Montevergine*. All 4 of these one-room chapels, in the Strait of Barba and on Partenio have a similar shape and none look like a tower. However, their shape is like the Heavens-Palace.

The website of *Santuario* says this chapel "looks like a tower" thus the name, but this is far from the truth. Archaic towers built around the world, especially round towers and turrets, represented the Axis on top of which is the Heavens-Palace of Polar Deities. The church has adopted these towers and built right next to them in so many places, for example, Ireland, that it's easy to think that the towers belong to the church. Instead, they had often graveyards here, being that the Tower is an Axis leading to the place of Immortality and all the Deities who can help a soul become Immortal.

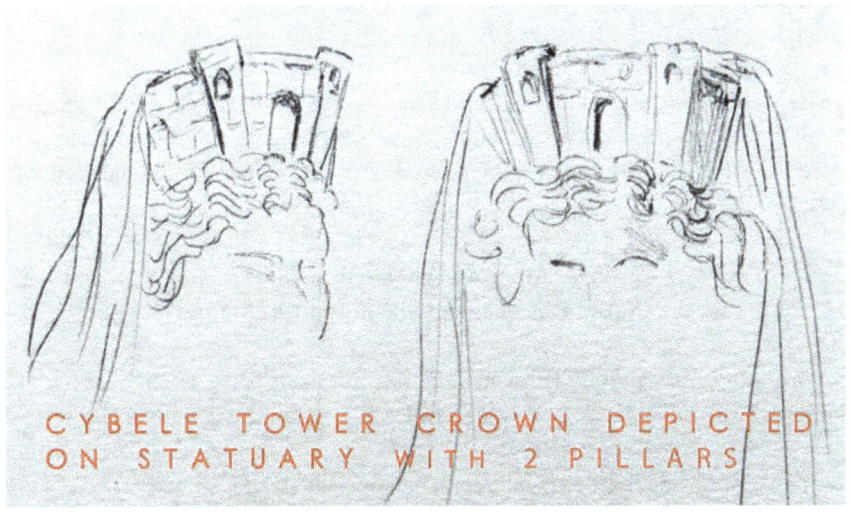

CYBELE TOWER CROWN DEPICTED ON STATUARY WITH 2 PILLARS

Cybele is connected to the Tower, long before any Madonna has been, because she is not only a Universe-Tree-Axis Deity, but because she dwells at the very top, as an Original Creator Deity, in the Heavens-Palace with all its exceptional power, its **Arcana** of secret knowledge, secrets of immortality, right to judge and to protect…This is why she is sometimes depicted wearing a **crown** that is a *Torrione*, and also with a Stone **Spear** (called **Pal** *as in the great Palatina of Ida*) which she has also been named. This means she is also envisioned as a stone Spear Deity who can mark the earth for center-points on which to place a sort of Omphalos.

So the Tower doesn't just represent a Connection point between heaven and earth, but also the Dwelling space of the Polar Deity, which usually is constructed with windows at the tower's top, just before the roof, facing the 4 cardinal points. These towers, as part of archaic oral beliefs around the world and as part of the Black Stone Mountain Polar worship beliefs, are both representatives of the Stone Axis of the Universe as well as the Heaven's-Palace located at the top: a form of the **Axis**, specified. Graveyards were built next to towers in ancient times as a means of support for the spirits leaving the physical world and traveling into the astral world.

While I'll be going into this more deeply in my next book, it's important to always note church bans on beliefs. Churches banned worship of: pillars, trees, dancing…and even towers. Churches were simply built next to pre-existing Towers and then changed the story through what I call PROXIMITY. Proximity is where a new ruling or governing body forbids the use of current beliefs and practices through adding lies right next to truths and reinforcing them, or the disobeying of the new rules, with punishments like exile or death. So, old towers were stolen by churches and given new uses and new gods, and it's the same with accessories of priests, etc. New myths must be made, new legends, that demonize the old gods, the old ways, so that fear runs through this whole process.

So it's possible there was also a tower built here when Cybele's temple existed, considering this history of other worldwide round towers. The 8 sided formation is used in these towers, as well, not separate from them, even if towers were mostly round, the 8-sided pillars and posts and the towers are both Axis symbols, with different specificities about the Sacred Motion they are related to, the Deities and aspects of Deity dwellings related to them.

Montevergine recap:
- Montevergine is inseparable from a Resurrection myth
- Its museum showcases a wooden zodiacal throne
- It features a large white stone Madonna and child which no one seems to talk about, though it's extremely odd to see this feminine representation in a church in this way and it's in the oldest part of this complex.
- **Madonna Nera**, the **Black Madonna** known as *Mamma Schiavona* in this location which takes us back to Cybele. But first....

Was Mamma Schiavona a slave,
just as Sarah was alleged to be in some of the stories?

No. Their stories are mythic templates referring to them being Highest of the High Divinely Feminine Beings who dwell in the Polar Center's Black Magnetic Mountain of Polar worship.

The words used to describe both Sarah, Mamma Schiavona and even Kali:
- **Black**
- *Schiavona*, from Neapolitan dialect = dark, dark skin, over time = slave
- **Kali** = dark, time, name of a Deity, but its etymological root **kar**, later **kal** mean: *to go, to drive* which brings us to our Black Magnetic Mountain words roots such as:
- **Ag**, **Ak**, **Ar** *to go, to drive, to urge,* that makes the cosmos turn round it.

Black Madonnas, *Madonna nera*, and other Divine Beings don't have skin, but they have associations with celestial zones and colors attributed to these zones, such as Black and white and red, which are very related to nature on earth, although it is believed all nature and earth existed first in the heavens.

For example, in the Chinese 4 Great Constellation groups, and others around the world we find they've been marked with colors:

Blue for the East- where all celestial bodies Rise-always used in water/resurrection stories
Black for the North - of our Magical, Magnetic Black Mountain and worldwide Black stone worship
White for the west, which is also North for these oral societies (based on the way the Milky Way rotates) and therefore the blazing white celestial light
Red is for the South, place of death, which alignment has been used in sacred burials...for example, head placed in the South so that it faces the Northern zone of Resurrection and Immortality.

These colors come from: Brightness of the Highest Heavens; Blackness of the most powerful magnetic stone in the Northern Cosmos that makes the entire universe revolve round it while it remains motionless, a sanctuary; and the Red of blood sacrifices and of a specific type of Resurrection: the soul's highest achievement of Immortality, which, incidentally, offers specific abilities to souls who achieve it as related to physical matter. Part of this cosmic zone also includes divine metals: gold, silver, brazen brass, and the entire Universe exists within the Celestial waters of creation.

Note: Madonnas and **Black Madonnas** are outfitted in very specific clothing: There are white statues with white veils and white bodies; There are dark blue veils with crowns of 12 stars, there are pale blue veils covered with stars or surrounded by stars, There are red veils coupled with blue gowns, and there are various Mountain-shaped veils covered with plants, vines, and Fleur-de-lis symbols.

Photos by Karyn Crisis. L-R: Triora, Napoli, Napoli, Sava

Mamma Schiavona

- one of the 7 Madonna** sisters
- the Sisters are Celestial figures which are of the Bears, that is the Ursa Major and Ursa Minor constellations, an integral part of Cosmic Polar Worship. The Pleiades are a forced connection here. They are not part of the Polar Creation story.

**For the true reveals of each sister, see my next books. Each sister is connected to a specific Celestial motion and symbol of the Polar zone.

The myths of Montevergine's **Black Madonna** reveal yet another mythical figure, Mamma Schiavona, referred to as *ugly, Black*. A Neapolitan song has been collected by Maestro Roberto De Simone in his collection "Rituali e canti della tradizione in Campania" that says of the 7 sisters:

> *"They are all beautiful*
> *except one who is ugly*
> *and therefore flees to a high mountain,*
> *Montevergine".*

These song lyrics tell us what to remember:
-ugly, Black
-high Mountain
…because according to tradition, the Madonna sisters were 6 white and one Black.

What is called "ugly, Black" ?
The heavens-fallen magnetic meteorites that have been venerated as Deity since archaic times.
What is on a high mountain?
Temples to Highest of the High Polar Deities who offer: Sanctuary, Stability, Neutrality of Judgement

and Unconditional love.
What do White and Black represent in the Polar Zone?
The turning of Night (which comes first) to Day, and the equal exchange keeping things in balance.
Why are there 7?
I have alluded to this with brief mentions of the Ursa Major and Minor constellations, and I'll be extending this information in my next book.

*Ugly and Black, ugly and dark, rugged...*is also how the Black meteorites fallen from heaven were described in document after document. Though it was acknowledged they were venerated as Deities of The Most High, not one description by observers was that these stones were beautiful; they were instead Powerful. So really we are being asked to remember the Black Stone Heaven's Mountain.

So, in the way Sarah was called *Sarah the Black,* the **Madonna nera** was called in the south of Italy in Naples and near other towns in Campania: Mamma Black, *Mamma Schiavona, la madonna brutta.* We can see Cosmic ideas encoded into simple memorable terms, which can also sound denigrating and racist without knowing first the context.

From travels in rural Italy, a truth is that in tight-knit villages, everyone watches everyone else and knows when someone different arrives in town. Anyone who is different from the townsfolk is looked at suspiciously, even when people are offering hospitality and kindness, and anyone different is often referred to as ugly. It certainly happened to me on one visit, where people were calling me ugly in the street, and one man even followed me into a cafe and yelled at me while I was eating my breakfast about how ugly I was. In another town during that month, a group of men surrounded me at a bar table while I was snacking and told me I was so ugly to have tattooed myself.

There's an emphasis on "us versus outsiders"...so when reading these mythic templates, it can be tempting to read earthly, human ideas into the stories. For example, *from the East* in earthly terms might mean someone from a country to the east of where someone currently is, whereas in mythic stories, local legends, and folk tales, East refers to the place in the sky where Heavenly Bodies arise, arrive, and are reborn. Divine Beings All are from the East. *Madonna Oriente* means refers exactly this.

At the same time, this Madonna of Montevergine / Mamma Schiavona / *la Madonna nera,* is described as *ugly,* she is also, according to another song collected by De Simone in his field research, referred to in this *esteemed* way:

> *"Oh Maronna, how beautiful you are,*
> *What are you doing in this chapel?*
> *What beautiful eyes that hold the Maronna,*
> *who seem to me like royal stars."*

After all, we are dealing with a Polar Deity here, who is in fact a royal star: the Polestar.
And, the Polestar Deity is is *Supreme Deity of the Night Heavens.* [164]

As with all Madonnas, for Mamma Schiavona too there are various myths and local legends. Unfortunately with these stories, people try to treat them as historical tales of earthly happenings and conceptualize their simple structure, and therefore disconnect them from their original source meanings (which weren't written down but instead envisioned and performed often as a ritualization of Celestial occurrences), turning them into stories about human beings. So then, with historicizing and referencing other writings, these older, once oral stories themselves become over-written by conceptual stories that are disconnected from a natural but encoded meaning, and they become edited, and eventually erased.

This happens because historians (and anyone reading the written records really) decide a myth or legend doesn't make a lot of sense in some parts, because we've lost the context, being that they were created by people using oral methods of keeping track of knowledge, which involves layers of symbolism, so we change the passages to make more sense to us, rather than trying to recapture the perspective and hidden knowledge that was written into it which made it sound weird in the first place. This has happened with a lot of myths, such as the ones mentioning floods and the ones about waters. As Dr John Knight Lundwall explains, myths from oral cultures were performed as somatic ritual in a group, and each person in a group had a layer of Knowledge and meanings connected to their actions. The time of year this ritual was performed had to do with its meaning…and all these things were known by Insiders, yet it was the Outsiders who tried to write them down…losing valuable information in the process.

Oral traditions are still practiced in Italy, and this is where these myths, rhymes with double meanings, and community Somatic Rituals have been handed down for generations. They have also been performed for generations, for so long that many layers of meanings have been lost, and yet the community rituals survive, along with the rural *guaritrici* medico-magical healer cures and their prayers and signatures (hand-markings). Still, since parts have been forgotten and parts seem nonsensical, they are often called "superstitious". These traditions hold the knowledge, they are the living links. The church knows this and has subsumed these beliefs and even traditions. It's widely known now among scholars that early christianity, before it was united by literate texts, was ritual-based just like mystery schools and other spiritual traditions. And dancing (and singing) was a way the secrets were taught to initiates.

===

MAMMA SCHIAVONA MYTH

As to Mamma Schiavona, described as the unconditionally loving *she who grants everything and forgives everything*, her myth is much more pointedly focused than this in her role as Divine Savior:

As the story goes, in 1256, two young gay men were kissing each other
and holding hands when they were attacked by the people around them.
The community, in judgement, stripped them of their clothes,
to make them even more vulnerable,
and tied them to a tree out of town
up on Mount Partenio (Monteverigne)
where they would be exposed to possible wolves, starvation,
whatever might come upon them in the night or days even, that followed.
Allegedly the Virgin arrived, untied them,
wrapped them in her mantle thus saving them,
and they lived happily ever after, creating a Miracle
that the entire community would have to digest.

If you read this myth carefully, you'll notice it bears a resemblance to the WATER myth templates, but the added specifics are: *Tree*, and *High Mountain*. While the water myths vary depending on precisely the celestial story being told, the template remains the same, details are plugged in. The general template:
- person or people
- danger confronts them
- a natural element is part of that danger
- they cannot save themselves from the danger. (Death is IMPLIED)
- a non-physical being helps them (IMPLYING THEY ARE IN THE ASTRAL)
- they are "resurrected" i.e. shown as SAFE and continuing on with their lives.
- the Mantle/Cloak is an important factor that is part of Cybele's story and part of the the Creation Stories found round the world…which I'm saving for the next book because explaining it lengthens this one too much.

In this Gay men oppression story and Resurrection Myth:
- 2 people facing danger:
- they are tied to a TREE,
- left to the elements on a MOUNTAIN TOP,
- stripped naked as to be even more vulnerable
- there are possible animal threats, exposure threats, starvation
- they cannot save themselves from this danger
- a Divine Being intervenes (the Virgin Mary here) and resurrects them
 - they continue on with their lives, being part of a Miracle.

Here, we have a Mythic Template, one that like the Water Myth is also found around the globe, where the Sacred Tree offers Sanctuary like the Black Stone Mountain does as well: they are on a High Mountain in this story, tied to a Tree. Remember our Black Magnetic Mountain is a sanctuary, it is stillness, everything else revolves round it, and the Tree Trunk is part of the Universe-Tree-Axis which Polar Deities (and Central Deities) use to move back and forth between the Cosmic spaces and the material earthly plane. Recall the Russian Fairy King myth about protecting children in the **Ax**is.

The mythic template here is about:
- the trunk part of the tree as the Universe-Axis of the Celestial Polar zone, instead of the astral waters of the Universe-Ocean,
- the Deity of the Polar zone, here as the Virgin Mary, who resides at the top of the Highest Celestial Mountain where the Heavens-Palace is supported by the Axis.

The Tradition of seeking Sanctuary and Protection from Polar Deities (and their Mantles/Veils and their Tree pole/post/axis) can be seen expressed through other cultures in a small sampling to follow, showing understand what's underneath Mamma Schiavona's myth:

First Nations People Kwakiutl and their view on the Milky Way
-This is a Winter Ceremony ritual that is a reenactment of a myth
-It takes place within a lodge* especially constructed for this ritual
-In the center of the lodge is a mast of cedar some 40 feet tall
that has been smoothed and it projects through the roof of the lodge
-A warrior is tied to this pole, this mast
-This mast is said to be the channel for spirits arriving from the otherworld

It is also referred to as a bridge to the sky
-It is named *Cannibal Pole*, and it is the *Man Eater's* own tree
that connects him with the sky
-This ritual is a reenactment of a myth about the Milky Way
-It is enacted by chiefs and warriors of the tribe, and the main role is of:
-*Man Eater* who is a Deity located at North end of the world and the headwaters of the
rivers which emanate there and is impersonated by the highest-ranking chief on earth. [165]
*It is believed there are lodges in the sky, which this ritual emulates.

- The *Udumbara-post* of the *Stapatha-brahmana* stood in the centre of the sacrifice shed; it was touched in the ritual, saying "here is stability, here is joy" as they grasp the pole.
The *Udambara-tree* is strength; they sit touching the *udambara-post*. They also form a circle round it, touch it, muttering the same mantra. [166]

- In the children's game resembling this called *Tig-touch-wood*, a child is safe from "catching" in the game when it's touching the wood. [167]

- Zakhariah the prophet is said by the Muslims to have taken refuge from his persecutors in the hollow of a tree. [168]

- Orestes taking refuge near the Omphalos was granted the same protection and security.[169]

- Enoch having, in Persian Muslim legend, got into paradise alive, refuses to be rejected and takes refuge near a Tree allegedly said that, *"unless the creator of paradise and hell removes, me, this place I shall not quit."* [170]

- References to Sanctuary provided by Polar Zones is expressed in these myths:
These myths are "seeking sanctuary by grasping the sacred tree" [171]

- **Ag**Dos, the Black centrally located Mountain stone is both part of the Black Magnetic Mountain and an Omphalos at once. Attis situs upon **Ag**Dos, and from it, Deukalion and Pyrrha took smaller stones and flung them down to earth to create humans. [172]

Note: Deities associated with the Pole because, as an Axis, it's envisioned as their transport from heavens to earth, zones which have separated (in our language we'd say that there's a difference, via perception) between physical realm and energy/astral/Celestial realm. The Pole (whether stone or wood, whether natural or carved into a pillar) has several meanings: A representation of the Deity who lives at the top of this Column in the Polar zone, so a Polar Deity or a Central Deity (several group types). Then there are Deities who can use this Axis to manifest on earth (a Deity "bursting forth from a Pillar, like **Ag**ni") There are poles/columns that mark entryways of special zones and portals, such as in front of the Heaven's Palace and its inner secrets, abilities, etc.

So while the stars are visualized by oral peoples as Dancing and dying/resurrection, the Axis, while it turns the universe, has an aspect of stationary quality to it, stability. The Black Mountain is entirely stable, and the axis turns on a pivot and other mechanical parts, but it belongs to the Polar Deities, the Spear gods and all those associated with columns, pillars, minarets, towers, tree trunks..and therefore is a place of protection by these Deities as well as.

The Mountain represents *High*, the highest height on earth parallel to the highest height in the universe. In comparison, Axis means *between heaven and earth* as well as *rotation*, where as Mountain is *fixed, still, constant*. Tree branches bear fruit: 12 zodiac paths for souls to have human experiences through; medicines from the leaves, and trance-inducing drinks from its nature: *soma, houma, graha*.

Components of the Somatic Rituals of Mamma Schiavona

"In oral societies, you dance the myth,
that's somatic narrative, you ritualize the myth...
you sing and dance memories that need to be passed down." [174]

Femminielli, who they are from an Italian perspective

Every year in Naples on the 2nd of February *femminielli* make a procession called *la juta* (the Ascent) *dei femminielli* from Naples to Montevergine on Mount Partenio to honor Mamma Schiavona the **Black Madonna** in her shrine on the mountain top 1400 meters above sea level at *Santuario Montevergine*. There is music and dancing, which is also a remnant of archaic Somatic Ritual with profound purpose.

According to older generations, *femminielli* are not just trans. They are different, even considered a 3rd gender by some. This is not my story to tell, but here are some notes from an Italian writer:

"The femminiello (little female) is a very important figure of the Neapolitan millenary culture. It is a male born person who identifies as neither a woman or a man. Femminielli [...] do NOT say they are women, they do not claim to be recognized as women." Due to this prerogative, the femminiello has always been a sacred creature, responsible for the administration of some rituals: when a child is born, he is placed in his arms as a good omen, one relies on him as a "celebrant" in group games that preserve the characteristics of the rite such as the Tombolata del Femminiello (from which men are strictly excluded) which refers to the Smorfia, the secret meaning of numbers. He is a direct descendant of the Coribanti, eunuchs consecrated to the Goddess Cybele, males who self-emasculated in the Dies Sanguinis and wore women's clothes to celebrate the Great Mother. The tradition of the femminielli is therefore inscribed in the cult of the mother, it is a tribute to the mother. Another ritual, the "litter of the femminiello" – who gives birth to a doll, the birth bed surrounded by her fellow creatures – imitates and honors female fecundity."* [175]

Reenactment of ancient Protectors of TRIAD Deity

An important part of this passage is the connection between Corybantes and Femminielli. Why? Because the role of the Corybante/ Kabeiroi/Galli/Salii and Dactyles was to protect the Triad Deity, of Cybele Attis, and **Ag**Disitis. Triads are also of the Polar Black Mountain Cosmic zone, the Highest of the High. They are a living link with the Polar rituals of the past.

Other living links are:
- Song and Dance, whirling, frenzy
- Procession and its circular nature, *which is a pilgrimage to the place of the teacher* for priests of the past, and in this case it's a pilgrimage to the Savior (see M Schavona myth)
- Wearing Cloaks/Mantles/Veils as some of the *femminielli* still do
- Triad symbols-the Corybantes had Fleur-de-lis tattoos. The Pansy is also a Triad symbol, which is of note here because *femminielli* have been called "pansies" in a way that is meant to insult their gender,

but Pansy is actually a symbol of the Highest of High Deities and their Priests.
- Music made of wooden castanets, drums and flute. The Flute especially, being an Axis symbol is perhaps the most important musical key connected to Cybele since it points to her dwelling on the Black Stone Magnetic Mountain.
- Song and dance as part of the Procession. In ancient times, these songs were called **Ax**amenta.
- **Axamenta** are ritual hymns, **Ax**is-Hymns, sung by the Salii and groups of Priests whose role was to guard the Buckler (Triad Deity).

These priests carried a lance/spear/staff (AXIS symbol, mimicking their Deity), wore a Conical cap (mimicking the Mountain) where their Deity dwells and wore a veil (representing the firmament). The songs they sang *"were in a speech so archaic that they had become incomprehensible, even to the Salii themselves in classical times"*. [176] The beginning of one:

> *Divom Dio exta cante,*
> *Divom Dio supplicante.* [177]

Recalling the Triad of: **Ax**iokersos, **Ax**iokersa, **Ax**iEros, who would be venerated through **Ax**amenata. These hymns were also part of rituals called **Thronosmoi**, which were rituals to the Great Mother Goddess involving Types of Dancing and Singing: initations, teachings of knowledge while mimicking movements of stars, dances where imitation of to-the-right rotation of the Cosmos is imitated, i.e. keeping the teachings alive.

It's said, in some accounts, that priests of Cybele were called Coyrbantes/Koribantes and in other accounts called Galli...and here is a reason names get interchanged: First, all these names: Corybantes, Cabires, Curestes, Dactyles, Salii and Galli (also spelled Korybantes, etc) *..these names were all plural and general, common adjectival names, not Proper names.*[178] *Femminielli* work the same way, a term for "little females", an adjectival name. So that's why it is said that one can be the other and yet fundamentally the same. They were ultimately keepers of secret knowledge who initiated others and passed on knowledge encoded in song and dance.

Mutilation of self: symbolic sacrifice for making new Divine Children

Corybantes were the Guardians of the TRIAD Deity...that was their role as priests, as well as to perform sacred dances that are meant to show forth the ***Harmonious March of the Heavens,*** like the dancing of the stars.[179] These groups were Veiled and Clothed in Purple*, which is a significant Celestial color. And, it is said that they also wore *pied*, that is *particoloured* robes, [180] which were so colored by the blood of self-inflicted strikes on each other from their swords, another sacrificial substitution. So the pied-piper multicolored clothing comes from this. *more about Purple, Veils and their significance in my next book.

The whirling howling spinning of dervishes was believed to be aout the Divine Motion around the Black Stone Mountain mimicking the howling certain Deities did from atop the Moutain Stone. The ancient castration ritual was a sacrifice and a mutilation like that of Osiris, which is always representative of a Deity cutting itself self into pieces for re-generaion, that is, to create Deities from their likeness.

The Somatic Ritual, *la juta dei femminielli,* involves:
- Procession

- Singing and Dancing
- and, since this was to a Polar Triad Deity, a sacrifice or simulacrum would be required in the past.

In processions and pilgrimages, the songs and dances still performed are survivals from archaic times, even with missing parts, from oral mystery schools that recorded Celestial knowledge and patterns into bodily actions and verbal group songs that are only to be performed as specific times so as to be remembered in specific ways. And, the simplest of details is often the most important. For example, particularly archaic is from field work by Roberto De Simone* in his words, *"can be traced back to devotion, that is, to the spiritual element that, linked to the myth, establishes a collective function."* And regarding traditions of *Mamma Schiavona according to Simone*:

"Popular songs cannot be performed by everyone.
Some devotees and pilgrims, in fact, can only accompany the rhythm or sing the refrain.
A particular characteristic of the songs dedicated to Mamma Schiavona
is that […] **they are sung by groups of 12****…and involve a pilgrimage."

** 12 is number of Zodiacal paths that as soul can choose from to pass into a physical body for the purpose of a life on earth in which it can potentially remember its own Divinity. So the 12 represents the 12 possibilities in the ecliptic.

In Mythic Templates around the world, the number 12 appears as "personas" such as 12 daughters or 12 sons or even as 12 stones laid in the earth in a circular formation that remind us of the circle of the ecliptic and its 12 paths.

Processional Song + Dance and Ritual Garments

In archaic somatic rituals, as Lundwall expresses as well, Dancing was a Medium, a way information was preserved through performance: on specific date, specific time, in a group where each person is somatically representing a layer of knowledge or information being transmitted.

- Pythagoras taught hard maths through song and dance and only to initiates.
- Pharaohs didn't invent the Pyramid Texts, they inherited them, but even they weren't texts, they were rituals and performances. [181]
- Italy is still full of these types of somatic rituals involving songs, dancing, group work.
- Herakles, of our the Water Resurrection Myths, was also called The Dancer in Egypt.
- Corybantes and Salii and the other male priests performed dance, many of which were 3-steps and circular, either broader circular such as starting in a place such as going to a pilgrimage point and then returning to the starting point, or they were performed as actual circular dances around the sacrificial poles and pillars, for example.
- In the Myth of Jesus and his 12 disciples in the Acts of St John, it is written as saying that Jesus says:

*"and whoso danceth not,
knoweth not what cometh to pass…
keep silence about my mysteries.
Unto you it is given to know
the mystery of the kingdom of god,
but unto them that are without,
all these things are done in parables."*

Meaning that only his "insiders" would know certain things, and others would be taught in generalities.
- In the Myth of Sophia in the Acts of St Thomas she is written to be giving secret hand signs to her 7 bridesmaids and teaching them the secrets of life through an initatory dance ritual. [182]

The Corybantes and others :
- often groups of 7 dancing 'round d the Pole, mimicking the Ursa stars dancing
- wore Conical caps, emulating the Mountain
- represent the Axis themselves, depicted as standing on one-foot
- Their dances were 'round, whirling (like dervishes) because the stars revolve around the Polestar

SKETCH OF WOODEN THRONE

2 PROTECTORS PERSONIFIED

2 PROECTORS AS LIONS

2 DIVINE BIRDS

2 PILLARS ON EACH SIDE

12 CIRCLES WITHIN ARE 12 ZODIACAL SIGNS

8 CARDINAL HALF-POINTS

3 SEATS: FOR TRIAD

THRONOSMOI

The Pietrosa Bowl/ Pietroasele Treasure is an artifact that only exists now in a diagram as a remnant of a spiritual mystery school. It depicts a round carved or embossed bowl at whose center sits and enthroned female figure, perhaps Cybele, or another Deity from the Black Stone Mountain at the Center of the Cosmos. There are figures embossed around the bowl itself depicting a Celelstial ascent in symbolic form, similar to the idea here about the 12 figures of the zodiac being possible paths for an embodied soul to take on its way to discovering its Divinity. The Pietrosa Bowl is more advanced than this, seeming to portray people already aware of their Divinity and moving deeper into the possiblity of Ascending to thier own Divine Thrones.

The THRONE added to the **Black Madonna** Mamma Schiavona painting and the wooden THRONE in the Museum have Somatic Rituals connected to them which draws us back to Cybele, the Great Mother Goddess rituals, and all the dancing priesthoods of: Salii, Galli, Corybantes, Cabires/Kabeiroi, Curetes, Dactyles, and even the *juta dei femminielli.*

Thronosmoi, enthronements in Rituals of the Mother of the Gods, were rituals practiced by the Priests of Cybele and other Polar Deity Triads. THRONOSMOI can be boiled down to very simple basics: The THRONE is the seat of Polar Deities residing in the Black Stone Mountain place of stillness, sanctuary, secret and sacred knowledge, and is the driving force of the Sacred Motion of the Cosmos that is in perpetual movement ROUND the Black Stone Mountain.

Thus, a person being initiated must imitate this by sitting on a throne while other initiates DANCE ROUND the throne, teaching the person the secrets they are inheriting on the throne via song and dance, whole they also invoke the Polar Dieties. The dancing round is the Right Motion of the Cosmos as well as the Dance of the Stars. The "unknown" element of the person being initiated is: will they in fact be given the secrets here on earth or will they have to be killed and receive them in the afterlife.

"Mother of the Immortal gods, …
Hail, Great Mother of Ida, Mother of the Gods!
Hail, O most ancient Sacred Goddess!
I offer you devout prayers, O Cybele,
You occupy the Central Throne of the Cosmos,
Wise of the Phrygians, the Ancient, Mother of Life, Tireless Lover,
Generous Goddess of Ida, You, Mother of Gods…
Now guide me in the years to come!
Goddess, make this a benign sign!
Walk beside me
with Your graceful step"

Left, man-made cave in Triora, Italy. Right, healing cave of the Goddess in Caserta, Italy.

CAVES

A widespread belief about the Milky Way found round the world is that in the Underworld is where all the knowledge about Healing exists, along with all the plants, even more than are found on earth, and that the healing process is likened to the process of death and rebirth. The Milky Way's Underworld is widely believed to have specific zones or areas for souls who are in-between lives, for example, but many other locales accessible by those who have the secret passwords to get through the gates and portals. So then, one area in particular that has been emulated on earth is: the Healing cave.

This is in the Southern Hemisphere of the Milky Way (which is also the East, because of the way the Milky Way seems to move in the sky). There is also a widespread belief that there exists a cave in the Northern Hemisphere, which is also the Western side, of the Milky Way, which is the zone of the Polestar, the Black Stone Magnetic Mountain and all that has been thus far mentioned about this High place, and that this cave is under the Black Magnetic Stone Mountain itself.

What is peculiar and interesting about the Healing cave is that, since it's in the Southern Hemisphere, the Divine Feminine half of the Milky Way, Deities from the Polar North must use the Axis to get down here, so in some cases they are considered *fallen*. The term *fallen* also means Deities who've been forgotten and replaced baby newer ones.

The Milky Way's Southern Hemisphere has a vast amount of spaces and locales, including the Galactic Center whose gates allows souls to become embodied in human flesh. But many associate the Underworld with "hell", and indeed in these beliefs there is a scary place in the underworld, but it's simply one part, not its entirety. In fact, the widespread belief is that in order to eventually reach the Northern Celestial Sphere of Immortality, each soul must pass through the Underworld anyway, to acquire more and more knowledge that assists this upwards evolution. Myths make it sound easy: one journey per human and, if successful, suddenly that human is immortal, when the reality is that many many lifetimes and evolutions back and forth between embodiment and as a soul in-bewteen are needed. I devle into Caves more deeply in my next book.

The tribes in the Paiute area he (Curtis, researcher) refers to as the Plateau Shoshone. In their tradition, the spirits of the dead are said to rise straight through the air to the Milky Way and travel southward to the end of the trail, where they find a lake with a **conical rock** *in the middle. Down through the hole in the apex of the rock they pass. At the bottom they emerge, living bodies, in Pugwainumu - muguwa - bitighan "Place where spirit goes in". Some say that below the Milky Way is another earth like this one of ours, but with more abundant grass and flowers. Tales from those who have died and returned say that one cannot see anything there. One hears the voices of people like the humming of "unnumbered flies".* [183]

SUMMARY

Black Madonnas or the Deities they have replaced have been part of Mystery School rituals of Ascension that are not part of christianity, honoring the Great Mother as a super-creator of the Universe, whose constellations dance round here, whose earthly natural symbols remind us of Her in Cosmic space, and whose Priests protect her Triad through dancing its knowledge as the stars dance round the Mountain.

Numerical repetitions still found in churches harken back to archaic usage, all describing Celestial zones and mechanical components of the structure of the Cosmic Mountain, its Heaven's Palace, its treasures and its timeless cross formed not by jesus, but from the emanation of the 4 Cardial Points issuing from the Black Stone Mountain.

CHAPTER 7: SEPARATION

THE SEPARATION of the HEAVENS + EARTH
Virgin Births
Madonna of the Vine
Ra Barca
Marriage of the Maggiolo and the Cima

===

"Heavens and Earth first parted,
and the 3 Kami performed the commencement of creation.
The Passive and Active essences then developed,
and the Two Spirits became the ancestors of all things." [184]
Japanese myth of Izanami and Izanagi, Original Creator Duo that formed a Triad

===

"Rangi and Papa,
Heavens and Earth the universal parents,
were one closely joined but were at length separated
by one of their children, the god of forests." [185]
New Zealand myth of Creator Duo who formed a Triad

Triads create Divine Children, i.e. souls who can become human and discover their Divinity through many physically embodied lifetimes. These Creator Duos can also create Divinities, gods and goddesses, directly from themselves, i.e. without those conscious beings having to go through physical embodiment and expansion until reaching higher and higher realms…like the rest of us.

The Separations of Heaven from Earth myths are integral to the idea of the Virgin Birth. The way these Myths are remembered is through:

- Mutilations personified heads cut off, body chopped into pieces, usually occurring between family members which are actually Deities and who are creating new Deities.

- Mutilations of plants cutting the beanstalk, the vine, the reed, river rushes.

- Disrupting transport taking away the ladder, removal of the boat, Death implied.

- As personified separations of doomed lovers, of spouses: separated by death or impossible circumstances.

- As Celestial Events envisioning the Milky Way as a masculine figure who creates the lights of the Northern Hemisphere and as a pregnant female figure who creates the lights of the Southern Hemisphere: the Virgin Births. Because the halves of the Milky Way were envisioned as gendered and separated, the Divine Feminine's stories of birth must envision her as impregnating herself or, as you'll see in myths, by Celestials. Virgin Births come from this visualization and observation. The interesting thing about the Milky Way's Southern Hemisphere is the Galactic Center, which you'll read about in the next chapter which actually does enable matter to be born without any assistance.

Myths from each category are presented here, and will reveal the truth of the Madonna of the Vine imagery. There are also myths and rituals that bring the Heavens back together with the Earth temporarily, which mimics remembrances of activity in Celestial space, such as in Somatic Rituals with trees where they are grafted back together: see the Somatic Ritual in this chapter from Accettura, Italy.

===

Mutilations in myth which tell the Celestial story
of the Separations of the Heavens from the Earth:

Castrations of Ouranos, Attis, Kronos and other male Deities are what was being mimicked by the Galli (and others) Priests of Cybele, which were in part a blood sacrifice, and clothing with blood spatter became part of the ritual (later represented by bright, multicolored patchwork veils), and in part a mimicking of the Masculine Deity creating new Deities from himself via "cutting chips off the ol' block".

Once Triad Deities came into being, which is a personified myth about Order coming form Chaos so as to "know thyself," this natural separation of a whole and united Being into separate parts was envisioned to occur for the Masculine and Feminine energies in all the Cosmos as well. So in the stories of masculine Deities where the Axis was referred to in a phallic way and it was severed, we are being asked to remember that the physical connection between the Heavens and Earth was changed and severed as well, so that the Creation of Deities and humans by Deities took on new Divine Motion.

From this separation of Locales or Zones in the Cosmos and then on planet earth, Celestial boats found their role, vines and bridges and reeds were venerated for their power to reconnect as an Axis for souls of humans. From this separation of wholeness into individual parts as: masculine and as feminine, new myths of Creation emerge due to a separation from what was envisioned as a Whole Being into separate parts who are still disembodied i.e. Deities, but who must create either Deities or humans separately rather than as a human masculine/feminine couple would through sexual intercourse. Thus, masculine Deities create via mutilations, and feminine Deities create through Virgin births.

Deities who have their heads chopped off are referring to this same idea: one part of the whole being permanently severed from the other. So that the physical connection between the the Entire Cosmos (the Body) and its ability to experience physical matter rather than the first form of Energy, is forever experienced now as a perception of separation (the Head) between the physical earth world and the Energy world of the Astral and all other Cosmic realms, spheres, etc. In myths about Divine Families personified, this is envisioned as Heads cut off, body chopped into pieces, usually occurring between family members which are actually Deities and not human beings.

===

Personified separations which tell the Celestial story
of the Separations of the Heavens from the Earth:

In New Zealand, the heavens and earth were regarded as a real pair...of bodily parts and passions, united in a secular embrace. But their 6 Divine Children wanted to experience the world outside their cosmic view and the strongest one who was the god of the forests, put his head against the earth and, with his feet against the skies, slowly pushed them apart ,* forever separating them. In other versions, he cuts the sinews that unite his parents, The Heavens and Earth, who cry in anguish at being separated cruelly. *This imagery is called a one legged Axis here, like Ptah and others to which I will expand on in my next book.

===

Mutilations of plants which tell the Celestial story
of the Separations of the Heavens from the Earth:

The Bean stalk: There are various mythic versions of Jack and the Beanstalk. In the English version, Jack's story tells us:

-There is a challenge. Jack and his widowed mother have a cow named Milky White (1)
who has stopped producing milk.
Jack decides to go sell the cow at the market.
-A man trades some magical beans for the cow,
promising Jack they'll grow high up to the sky. (2)
-Jack goes to sleep in the attic (3), waking to find the beans have indeed
grown a stalk that goes High high up into the sky.
-He climbs the stalk like a ladder 3 times, each time avoiding being eaten by the Giant (4), and each
time he brings back something golden: (5)
The 1st time gold coins,
The 2nd time a hen that lays golden eggs,
The 3rd time a golden harp.
-After the 3rd time he avoids being eaten by the Giant, he chops the beanstalk,
severing it as the Giant topples down and dies(6)
- Jack and his mother continue living an abundant life.

(1) Reference to The Milky Way
(2) The Heavens, an Axis
(3) Replicating the Heaven's-Palace on the Mountain, invoking the Highest point
(4) Central-Heavens Deity

(5) Robbing the Heaven's Treasury/Arcana which holds highest Celestial secrets
(6) Separation of the Heavens from the Earth

The Pea stalk and Cabbage stalk: There are various versions of the Pea stalk and Cabbage stalk in a Russia: Parents are mentioned here instead of a young Russian boy and called the Old Couple (1) whose story revolves around a cabbage stalk, in others as a pea stalk.

The basic myth components:
-The Old Man is climbing up the Pea stalk or the Cabbage stalk
-He carries The Old Woman on his back or in a sack
-She falls from his back or he throws down items he's gathering from above onto her and She then falls back down to earth, breaking into pieces and dies, or she is torn into pieces as well. (2)
-In all versions, the stalk breaks under the weight, and we are told,
"Since that time, no one has set foot in that heavenly cottage izbushja (3); so no one knows anything more about it." [186]

(1) This refers to the Original Creator Duos of the Black Stone Magnetic Mountain and the titles of "Old Man, Old Woman" appear round the world with this association.
(2) The Separation: both the fall AND the bodily mutilation, death, and breaking of the stem
(3) The Heaven's-Palace and its Arcana of treasures

The American Mandan tribe of the Great Plains who have lived for centuries primarily in what is now North Dakota, and now part of the Three Affiliated Tribes or Mandan, Hidatsa, and Arikara Nation, had a myth that *the tribe climbed up a vine from the underworld to the Earth, but when half have ascended the vine breaks with the weight.* [187]

The Golden Vines of myth then,
are the veneration of the connection between the Heavens and earth…
rather than a reminder of its separation.
The stem of the vine is an Axis, just as it is with the Reed and River Rush.
===

Myths of the Separations of the Heavens from the Earth
as Celestial Events

"The Samoan heavens at first fell down and lay upon the Earth until the arrowroot and another plant, or the god Ti-iti-i pushed the heavens up." [188]

"The Egyptian idea that the (feminine) heavens came down and lay upon the Earth all night until Shu lifted her up each morning. Sky was Nut, Earth was Seb." [189]

So bands of stars, as the Milky Way, and strips of sky along with plants and soil and light were all personified into stories together in memorable ways, recalling observations of heavenly happenings.

CHAPTER 7: SEPARATION

===

**The Separations of Heaven from Earth
resulting in Virgin Birth myths:**

So then, the Virgin Birth story comes from none other than the story of the halves of the Milky Way, explained through worldwide myths of a husband and wife (or in some cases, twins) forced to separate, wherein the female remains a perpetual Virgin. And yet, both halves create Divine Children. For example:

- New Zealand myth: *Rangi* and *Papa*, Heavens and Earth the universal parents, were once closely joined but were at length separated by one of their children, the god of forests. [190]

- Greek myth: The Virgin *Kore* in myth gives birth to *Aeon* on January 6 coinciding with Epiphany.

- Mexican myth: *Chimalma* the wife of *Mixcoatl* (cloud-serpent) finds a *chalchihuitl* stone in sweeping, swallows it, and becomes miraculously pregnant of Quetzalcoatl (feather-serpent). [191]

- Irish myth: *St Kieran's* mother had a dream that a star fell into her mouth. She asked Druid priests to interpret this dream and they told her she'd give birth to a son who'd become famous for his virtue.

- Chinese myth: *Chang Tao Ling* was born of a virgin mother who dreamt that the Polestar descended and offered her a sweet-smelling herb; on waking, a divine odor filled the room, and she was with child; she was delivered of him on the heavens-Eye-mountain, called *tien-muh sham*.

- myth of *Mary*: she was impregnated by a ghost called *the holy spirit* in the Christian story, and this spirit told her betrothed husband, Joseph, that the baby would be a boy and this son would save people from their sins.

Triad in Napoli, photo by Karyn Crisis

The belief in the Separation of Heavens and Earth is also why separate spiritual practices and activies for men and women exist in societies: whether Mystery schools only for men and Mystery schools only for women, masculine and feminine "sides" of buildings and zones, and also why in small villages in Italy it's common to see old men hanging outside the Bar sipping espresso, while on the side streets outside their homes are the women, partaking in town gossip and sharing recipes and remedies.

I used to take it personally, but it makes sense that since this belief about Cosmic structure exists, then on earth too it will, since earth is replica of Cosmic space and its structures mark the Heavens on Earth.

===

Myths of the Separations of the Heavens from the Earth
Personified as Separated Lovers/ Forbidden Marriages
performed as Somatic Rituals: *ra Barca*

There are 2 Somatic Rituals of Italy which contain these myths. One we'll examine from the North and one from the South. The one from the North tells of the separation. The one in the South tells of the reunification.

Somatic Rituals, here of Italy: North
- telling the story of a couple in love, forever separated and commemorated through a wooden ship mast from Bajardo, Liguria, (northwestern) Italy

Somatic Rituals, here of Italy: South
- telling the story of a masculine tree and feminine tree reunited through marriage, from Accettura, Basilicata (southeastern) Italy

Flyer for ra Barca, and next to it, the Barca pole lying on the ground, Bajardo, Italy. by Karyn Crisis

Ra BARCA of BAJARDO

In 2006, while not the first time I'd traveled to Italy, it was the first time I went to live among locals and travel around in small villages. I witnessed some of the the preparations for *ra Barca*, the somatic ritual in Bajardo that is still practiced every year. (see my photo of the flyer). Bajardo is medieval village that stands at an elevation of 3,000 ft on a Mountain peak in the province of Imperia in the region of Liguria in Italy.

What I saw was an enormous tree trunk that had been stripped of branches and had been pulled to the town center *centro*. Men were digging a hole in the middle of the paved street in which to plant this *Barca*. They were preparing to perform the *ra Barca* Somatic Ritual and its myth.

Key symbols of this myth:
- 3 daughters (Triad)
- cut wood, tree pole (Axis)
- sailor (reminding us of Celestial waters)

- the number 8
- lovers killed/death/the Challenge
- mutilation (head chopped off)
- Pentecost: 50 days of resurrection/rebirth
- astral boat (in song lyrics reminding us of the Boat of souls between Heavens and Earth)
- month of May (when Heaven comes down to Earth)
- singing and dancing (to perform the encoded knowledge as a group)
- remembrance through community ritual
- nobility (a reminder of the Holy North, its Polar Deities and Triads)

The myth is:

There was a noble family of 3 daughters.

In 1241 (which equals 8, the half-cardinal points which often are used to refer to the Cosmos and the Heavens) a sailor comes to the local woods to choose trees for building an imperial fleet of ships. One of the daughters falls in love with this sailor, and he invites her to follow his ship *ra barca*. They flee together into the woods on a path still remembered as "lovers' path". The noble father protests and he cuts off his daughter's head to prevent this union and he displays it in the center of town. In other stories, both are executed by men hired by the father.

A choice selection of the song lyrics that reveal the separation between Heavens and earth:

In Part one, the story is recalled:

"*Ra barca*/the Boat: *This night goes away! Let go, daughters, she will soon return, ah! He will return soon! Go ahead and take turns, In a boat on the sea it can never sink, ah! It can never sink! The port where it arrives, it is a good port, it will be good for the Lady! And whoever takes us there, it will be very nice, He is a good Master! The master who handles it, has taught it well, ah! He has taught it well! The first to greet, he would be my lover, And there are the three daughters of a Count, All three on the balcony ... well, well!*"

In the Third Part, called Complaints, the Challenges are recalled:

Daughter: *Father, have mercy on us. That I would let myself go to the garden [to meet my lover], Father, let me go to the garden!*" Father: "*Ask for the grace I would like, But I don't want you to go to the garden, but I don't want you to go to the garden!*"Daughter: "*My father would beat me and kill me.*" Father: "*Daughter Angelina come home!*" Daughter: "*Father, if thou beat me, why smitest thou me? Batei is dressed in seven crowns!*" [here, the 7 refers to the Polar Constellations of the Ursa Major and Ursa Minor and the 7 realms of Ascension achieved resulting in the Crown]

In the Fourth part, the Drama is recalled: The first blow that the he [the Father] gave, The head on the ground it killed!

In the Finale, a recap: "*ra barca/ The Boat, This boat of my love is going away this night! It's going away!*" *All song lyrics source:* [193]

The Somatic Ritual of Remembrance that is performed:

The performed Ritual takes place on Pentecost, in May, which means "50", and refers to the 50 Helpers who assist a soul in Ascension. The Sunday before Pentecost, a pine tree is chosen, it is stripped of its bark and branches and is taken back to the village. *At the top, a branch is cut and joined with a rope at the top to represent Angelina's head*

136

The pole, representing the *Barca* Boat is planted in the town *centro* center, round which the dances and singing will take place. *The entire village takes to the square to "girà 'ra barca": everyone holding hands turns clockwise and anti-clockwise around the tree, which is always taller than twenty meters, intoning the long song that is made up of different parts* [as recapped above]. *This is the oldest popular festival in the Ponente.* [194]

===

Bringing the Heavens back together with the Earth
The Somatic Ritual of :
Maggio **in Accettura, Italy**

Used with permission of Manchester Univeristy Press from "Sonic Ehtnography: When the trees resound: Towards a sonic ethnography of the Maggio festival in Accettura" by Lorenzo Ferrarini and Nicola Scaldaferri, Article and Book, Copyright 01/01/2020; permission conveyed through Copyright Clearance Center, inc.

The ritual of *Maggio,* which enacts the reconnection of Heavens and earth, takes place in late May to early June in Accettura, Italy.

Significant factors of this Ritual:
- 3 Day Fest, TRIAD, nod to the Celelstial North
- <u>Tree marriage</u>: physical grafting: *Cima* BRIDE and *maggio* GROOM. *Cima* refers to the Tree Top and *Maggio* refers to the Tree Trunk
- <u>Trees decorated</u>: A *Cima* upended is the same as an *Asherah* which were highly decorated

- <u>Procession of a statue</u>: In the case of Accettura, however, a male saint was injected with religious ideas in 18th century to this already enacted ritual
- <u>Music and Song</u> accompanying the gathering of the tree parts as well as the remembrance
- <u>1st Sunday in May after Easter</u>: celestial happenings
- <u>Pentecost</u>: what it means: 50 days
- <u>Ascension Thursday</u>: When the Deities return to the Heavens, 1st Sunday after Easter
- <u>Oxen</u>: will be discussed in my next book along with animal groups
- <u>Trunk of Tree</u>: (male, bottom) joined with leafy part of Holly (top, female)

This Somatic Ritual takes places in Accettura, Basilicata, Italy. The whole community participates:
- groups of men, called *maggiaioli*, who gather the *maggio* tree of Oak which will be the Groom (as the pole), with oxen
- groups of women called *cimaioli*, who find the *cima* tree of Holly (as the top) which will be the Bride;
- people guiding the oxen to pull the trees through the forest and then to remove the branches (of the maggiolo)
- people decorate the *Cima* like the *Asherah*, which was decorated with metal tags, formerly cheeses, meats, animals and animal parts
- people who sing and play music to accompany this somatic ritual, with words full of secret meanings of celestial movements that are being reenacted on earth: the marriage, or reconnection of the Separated Heavens and Earth.

- Monday is traditionally called *Whit Monday*, meaning *Descent,* in some places where Ascension rituals are celebrated. And for this *Maggio* festival, Monday is the day when the preparations are made to plant the *maggio* in town, to make its descent from the forest and touch down on earth: the center of town.

- Tuesday the tree parts are joined, after which there are songs and dancing.

- Ascension Thursday is the day when Deity ascends back to Heavens…though this traditional day has been changed to Sunday, and with the *Maggio* festival, on Sunday the *Maggio* and *Cima* who are now grafted together, are taken down.

This ritual takes place around Pentecost which means "50", reminding us here of Lundwall's discoveries like: *Gilgamesh where part of his journey he has to travel through 7 mountains and pass an impassable sea and is given 50 HELPERS that sparkle in the SKY, and these 50 are led by 7 LEADERS sphinx-like (leonine features wings of eagle) who pass through 7 gates with 7 guardians in 7 spheres in order to Ascend. Lundwall found these 50 Helpers in every mythological tradition in the old world and always in the same context: to Ascend, a soul must have 40 Guardians to pass into the Underworld. The purpose of the Underworld descent is to then rise/Ascend to Heaven.* [195]

===

Photo by Karyn Crisis

VINE
*"Erigone was also said to be the vine,
climbing and hanging on the Trees"* [196]

So then the vine, also as the golden vine in myth, is an example of the Axis, the ladder the CONNECTION between heavens and earth un-severed. And this applies to Deities decorated with the vine, that they are Helpers/Ladders/Columns/Axis to help us Ascend. Ascension in the Traditional sense is only for Souls however, not for human beings. The concept that human beings can Ascend right now in this present life while still in the same body…this is a new social-media definition of Ascension which is not actually possible.

SUMMARY

The **Black Madonnas** or the Deities they replaced are newer versions of an older feminine Deity, pre sun-worship, pre moon-worship, of the Southern Hemisphere of the Milky Way, where the Underworld and is.

The idea of a chaste Goddess has nothing to do with sex and only with the envisioned separation of the Masculine and Feminine halves of the Cosmos. Myths then tell the story of the Separations of the Heavens and Earth through imagery of vines, reeds, cords being cut, along with myths about married partners or lovers being separated, in ways that make it impossible for them to be together, similar to the idea of the impossible Celestial seas for a human being to cross while staying alive in a human body.

Processions tell these stories and reenact both the Descent and Ascent of Deity.

CHAPTER 8: 12 STAR CROWN, Galactic Center

12 Star Crown
Zodiac Ecliptic
Galactic Center: The Sun's Sun
Moon Crescent it's not

Photo: by Karyn Crisis.
Imagine instead of the 12 stars, the 12 zodiac Animals or signs, as the Ecliptic circle of time.

Crowns as circles of time, symbols of authority…and here, as symbols of the Creator of souls who can pass into the earthly realm. When the zodiac intersects with the Silver Gate of man, souls can pass from Creator Deities into a path for one of 12 possibilities for a physically embodied earth life, wherein that soul has the possibility to remember its Divinity through trials and challenges and experiences only available in the physical world…wherein all the laws of energy apply, but are hidden behind the illusion of slow-moving physicality.

Maja "sent her son from high"…[197]

The 12 Star Crown is a symbol of a Creator Deity who can use Galactic Gates to allow souls of man to return to astral space as well. Only Divinities can operate this gate and only specific ones. And, the 12 Star Crown is a symbol of a Triad Deity who can assist souls ready for Ascension to the Highest

Realm of Immortality, such as Mythic Characters mentioned in this book, which is accessible through the Golden Gate of gods into that Realm. The 12 stars represent the 12 zodiacal signs on the ecliptic.

12 Star Crown Deities are also Ascended Masters, who can use the Golden Gate to return to earth with the most recent physical body they inhabited rather than be born as a baby and grow in an earthly life: instead, they return to earth as an already established Identity. This Gate is located towards the Galactic Center between the Sagittarius constellation and Scorpius constellation.

The Galactic Center is the Pregnant belly-looking ball of light that also contains an expansive Black hole within the Milky Way's Southern/Eastern hemisphere, the half attributed to the Divine Feminine. This massive Black hole doesn't devour energy but instead expands matter outwards. It is surrounded by a central bulge of old, yellow stars, after which lanes of blue stars spiral out. It's the Cosmic Womb. This is really what is celebrated Dec 21-25: not the sun returning, but the sun's orbit through the zodiac that passes near the Galactic Center, where the Gates are: it's an open-portal moment on the clock of the solstices.

The Golden Gate is the gate of gods, a gate that *makes humans into gods* through its portal to Immortality* and towards the Galactic Center as the "Crown of Heaven", the highest achievement. The guardian of this Gate is Antares, a Red supergiant massive star, several hundred times the diameter of the sun and 10,000 times the Sun's luminosity, the brightest star in the constellations Scorpius and one of the largest stars visible to the naked eye.

"And on this side of the River and on that was a Tree of Life bearing twelve crops of fruit, yielding its fruit every month. And the leaves of the tree were for the healing of the nations."*
*Implied: north side of Heavens-River [198]

This is where the Tree of Life inferences comes into Cosmic Structure: that Creator Deities dwell at the TOP of the Tree, versus the Axis and the Roots, and here, at the Top of the Tree is where we find created by them:
- Leaves and literal fruits as Medicine, recalling the Native American belief that all plants and animals exist in Cosmic space, in greater abundance and type than on earth
- Nature's flowers (Fleur-de-lis and other white flowers) which, when combined properly, make **Mag**ical drinks that can open one's consciousness to the Secrets of the Cosmos (kept in the Arcana of the Black Stone **Mag**netic Mountain)
- the 12 zodiacal paths (and its 12 animals, the 12 types of humanity which can be embodied) also envisioned as the 12 fruits.

In myths then are also found the usage of 12, often as 12 brothers or 12 stones set in a circle who represent the Zodiac, and in Somatic Rituals we also find 12 people, such as 12 people to perform a Pilgrimage or song, or groups of 12 priests like the 12 Bucklers of the Salii. Within the Black Stone Mountain there are also the 12 thrones of 12 judges in Black caps, the Athenian altar to 12 gods was in the **Agora** [199] and as a last note of too many to list, the 12 peers of Charlemagne and of France were 12 equals of the Round Table. [200]

"Sveigder made a solemn vow to seek Godheim, the home of the gods, and Odinn the Old. He went with 12 (zodiacal) men through the world, and came to Tyrkland. He came to a mansion called Stein where there was a stone as big as a large house. Sveigder[...]saw a dwarf standing in the door, who called to

him to come in and he should see Odinn. Sveigder ran into the stone, which instantly closed behind him, and he never came back." [201]

This myth should bring to mind other Deity myths of those who became engulfed in tree trunks or earth. Here, Sveigder becomes a stone, meaning that he has also become a Stone Deity himself. The rest of this story alludes to him at the House of the Gods i.e. the Black Stone Mountain behind its Heavenly Gates. The number 12, representing the 12 zodiacal paths, are meant to remind us of the soul's work in each life which is to acquire knowledge for eventual Ascension through the Golden Gate into Immortality.

===

Unfortunately, the sun is misattributed in many myths…keeping the truth far away.
In art, the heavenly spheres are mistaken for the sun and the "sun disc"; horses are imagined to be "pulling the sun around" rather than the Galactic Center…and these attributions have been made to cultural symbols during time periods where those cultures didn't even acknowledge the sun and especially the moon in that way.

Round the world, Milky Way creation stories are nearly identical along with beliefs about its structure and offerings. And yet, sun and moon beliefs widely vary, mostly because the sun and moon were not considered to exist at beginnings of creation, and were believed to be inferior celestial bodies when they did appear/were created. The alleged Moon Crescent that many a Madonna can be found standing on is not the moon at all but rather the crescent of the Southern Hemisphere of the Milky Way which contains the Galactic Center, the "pregnant belly".

===

The Triad of Mary, Joseph and baby Jesus and the Manger Story features these symbols: animals in the Manger (zodiac symbols), The guiding Star (Pole star), the 3 wise men **Magi** (Triad from Black **Mag**netic Stone Mountain), December 24th (Galactic Center, when new Divine Children are made).

===

SUMMARY

Black Madonnas or the Deities they replaced, wear garments that represent Celestial spaces, Portals, Gates, Constellations, the Zodiac Ecliptic and other Celestial bodies. She is our 12 Star Crown Deity who works the Gates and births the Zodiacal 12.

CHAPTER 9: GATES

The Gates: notice the Cornucopia, Flowers with 8 petals, Flowers with 6 petals, and Birds
(which are an important part of my next book).

A grand culmination of this exploration brings us to the earthly Heavenly-Gates in Italy, and surely there are Heavenly-Gates around the world as well. These Gates are not just symbolic, they are an actual Portal, complete with Protectors-in-Spirit and reported phenomena. The Gates are located (one set, in Avellino) specifically at *Chiesetta Madonna della Pieta*, the one room church with the 2 trees in front of it in the Mountain strait of Barba across from the river Sabato that is ever-present in witch tales of the Campania region. This is also why the Walnut Tree of Benevento story is focused here…but that is a tale for my next book.

In this community around these gates, reaching through Avellino, Ceppaloni, Chianchetelle, and even to Benevento, the locals both fear and respect this locale. There are a lot of stories, legends, and rumors about *Chiesetta Madonna della Pieta* with the Gates particularly, but also about the entire area, which Carlo Napolitano calls in his book *"il triangolo stregato, il mistero del noce di Benevento"*, The Bewitched Triangle, the Mystery of the Walnut tree of Benevento". He shares many of these stories and his own personal experiences in his book, and, as a result of him taking me to spend time here, I've also written about some of my experiences in my first book, "Italy's Witches and Medicine Women."

At the time Napolitano was researching his book, he had discovered that the 3 churches mentioned previously in this book (and are featured in his) form an obtuse triangle, with its center point (somewhere around 90-120 degrees) pointed at the *Chiesetta Madonna della Pieta's* Gates. He writes of his belief that they are protective charges of the land area, which is something that can palpably be felt along the haunted road SS88 that goes through this Mountain Strait of the *stretto di Barba*.

When I met Carlo years ago while in Italy interviewing people for my fist book (that I didn't yet know was becoming a book), he brought me to this area around the Sabato river among the triangle of odd churches to set foot in front of all 3 plus the one in Chianchetelle outside of which are the pillars and statue mimicking *Chiesetta Madonna della Pieta*'s structure and hidden meaning. He let me stay at *Pieta* at midnight on 2 occasions alone, and waited for me while I scaled down the cliffside to the Sabato river bank. He told me that here the Divine Feminine had touched down physically.

Well, it turns out he was correct indeed. He hadn't as yet solved the mystery…but a passage in another one of his books that he gave me helped light the way for this book: "*Il guardiano di Pietra. Sulle tracce del sabba e della grande madre nel Sannio Campano*"/The Guardian of Stone on the Trail of the Sabbath and the Great Mother in Sannio Campano", oddly, because I've not had time to translate it, sadly, after all these years. However, during last year's gloomy, rainy winter, while wishing I was in this area in Italy, and while working on this book, I found myself thumbing through its pages. I stopped on a particular page, which had a photo of the *Chiesetta Madonna della Pieta*. I decided to translate this page because I felt it buzzing with mystery. On This page Carlo wrote about a statue of the Madonna being taken from inside the *Pieta* and moved to another church in Chianchetelle: *Chiesa di Santa Margherita*, and he wondered why. Then, so did I. The answer is here in this chapter.

So I asked too, why does the statue move? Why are people moving it? Is there are official Procession? What does the *Chiesa di Santa Margherita* look like? In fact, this *Chiesa* is very large and in a more accessible area than the 3 mysterious ones in near the Sabato river. It's also the one that features the hidden-in-plain-site depiction of the Heavenly-Gates, which then makes sense that it would be a "partner" church to *Pieta*.

I decided to translate a few pages on either side of this page. I saw Carlo had written "Queen of Heaven", a term I'd heard before, but what does it really mean? Why is she Queen of Heaven? Well, according to all the symbols that **Black Madonnas** and Madonnas have been accessorized with in statuary and in paintings, we find all the Authority symbols fo the Polar North zone, that is, a Soul who has become Immortal, meaning, Immortalized as a specific Identity (versus the Immortality we all possess simply because we have souls), such as: 50 Helpers, Water myths, the Polestar, associations with the unmoving Sanctuary and stability of the magnetic Mountain, the element of iron, the snow and rain and milk, the pomegranate, the Fleur de lis and the ivy and pansy, Crowns (of time, of the ecliptic as the 12 stars crown, so as Ultimate creator of souls and humans), Pillars, Gates, Spears, Axis and the Throne, Ursa Major and Ursa Minor connections, clothing that resembles Mountains and is covered with plants and flowers…Processions with dancing and music, commemorations of Separation of the Heavens and Earth, and the rituals of Ascended Masters returning to earth, as are featured in this chapter.

That's when I re-read a page I had translated of this book of Carlo's that I didn't pick up before because I simply had focused on the movement of the icon from church to church…What I read delighted and shocked me: "*in the church of Santa Margherita in Chiancetelle, inside there is another statue, which takes us to the theme of Mary suffering from the death of her son: virgin of sorrows, clearly recalling, in her Black dress, the Goddess Isis image of the Black Virgin…*" [203]

I wasn't able to find an image of this statue and I didn't visit this church, but it's clear that the Black dress is symbol of the NORTH, not of sorrows, the place of the **Mag**netic Mountain and yes, wherein dwells the Mother of Gods of any culture and every culture.

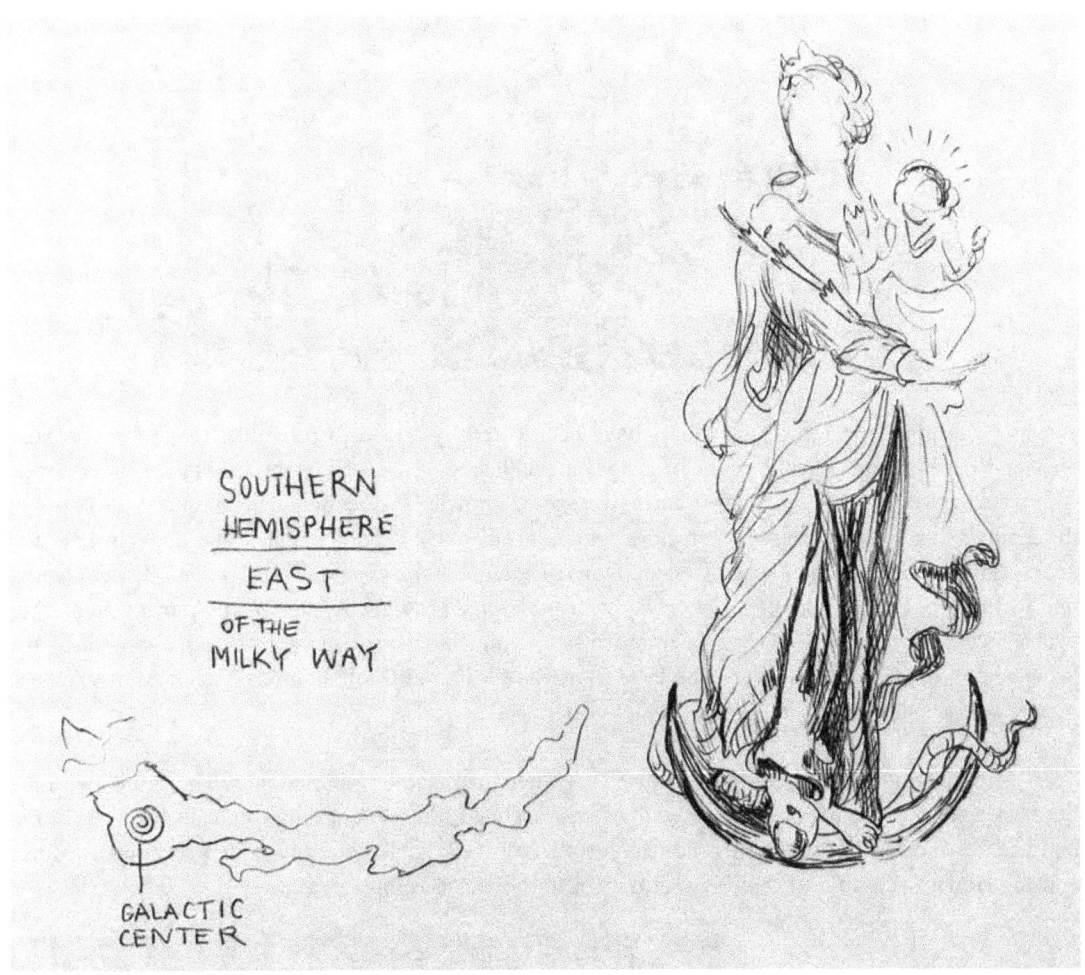

This sketch contains Celestial symbols that hint at what's hidden in plain site in *lo stretto di barba*, The Sabato River runs through this area, right alongside one of the churches as it passes through the strait, Mountains on either side forming a sort of Southern Hemisphere Milky Way crescent shape, and at the bottom or deepest part of its gentle slope can be found: *Chiesetta Madonna della Pieta,* just like imagery showing her stepping on her Hemisphere. The serpent represents the Milky Way, and the egg it has in its mouth is where the Triad Deity separated itself from.

What is represented in the photo of stone objects, in short, is the *Happy Heavens Gate* referred to in many poems, such as the ones that have been shared in this book where the Virgin Mary and the Black Madonna is likened to the Polestar. This statue, in the center of 2 pillars that resemble trees, is a twin of *Chiesetta Madonna della Pieta* where there is the church (where the Madonna descended, in a Mountain strait, as a physical being, and then Ascended once again to the Polar Zone) and the 2 trees/pillars in front of it, which represents: Gates of Heaven and its Guardians. The Heavens-Gates are a Portal to Polar Deity dwelling: and all is treasures and secrets.

The plants on top of the pillars have been carefully added to resemble trees tops…because Heaven's Gates are not just part of the Axis, they are at the top of the Axis, at the top of the Universe tree, where are the fruits (souls), medicines and secret sacred knowledge. Keeping that in mind in the photo of the 2 pillars that Pillars represent protectors, and pillars also mark: portals, gates, and doors in Celestial zones. Pillars also represent Deities who are twins *of each sex: one male and one female, such as Gemini and Castor and Pollux, and other sets of twins in myth joined at the back and then separated, and after which they keep on opposite sides of a doorway.* Gemini has long been considered a symbol of the Protectors of the Gates of Heaven. The Ursa Major and Minor constellations are the Gates themselves, as they also are like mirror-images of each other.

In the middle, the body of the Polar Deity, here depicted as the Madonna. The church with the trees: that is her place of Descent to earth as an Ascended Master returning to physicality, where her body comes back and forth to earth and why her statue is taken out and put back in, to remind us **of her coming Down to earth and then her return Up to the Cosmos once again.**

The doors of the *Pieta* open to the East, so as her icon is moved from the western part of the *Chiesetta* out that door, she is reborn, and then she is moved to the church in the East in Chianchetelle, where she will stay and slowly sink into the Underworld as the Milky Way's Galactic Center gradually disappears below the horizon line "in death" and slowly moves west again as she returns to Cosmic space, taking her body then turned-to-light, to Ascend once again during a process of months which then finds her returning to earth as the Galactic Center becomes visible in the Springtime once again where she'll return to earth...and then will begin the grand cycle again. Or more correctly, the cycle will be performed on earth for her.

So as her wooden statue is moved to the Chiesa in Chianchetelle, this symbolizes her return to being housed again in the Celestial Heavens-Palace.

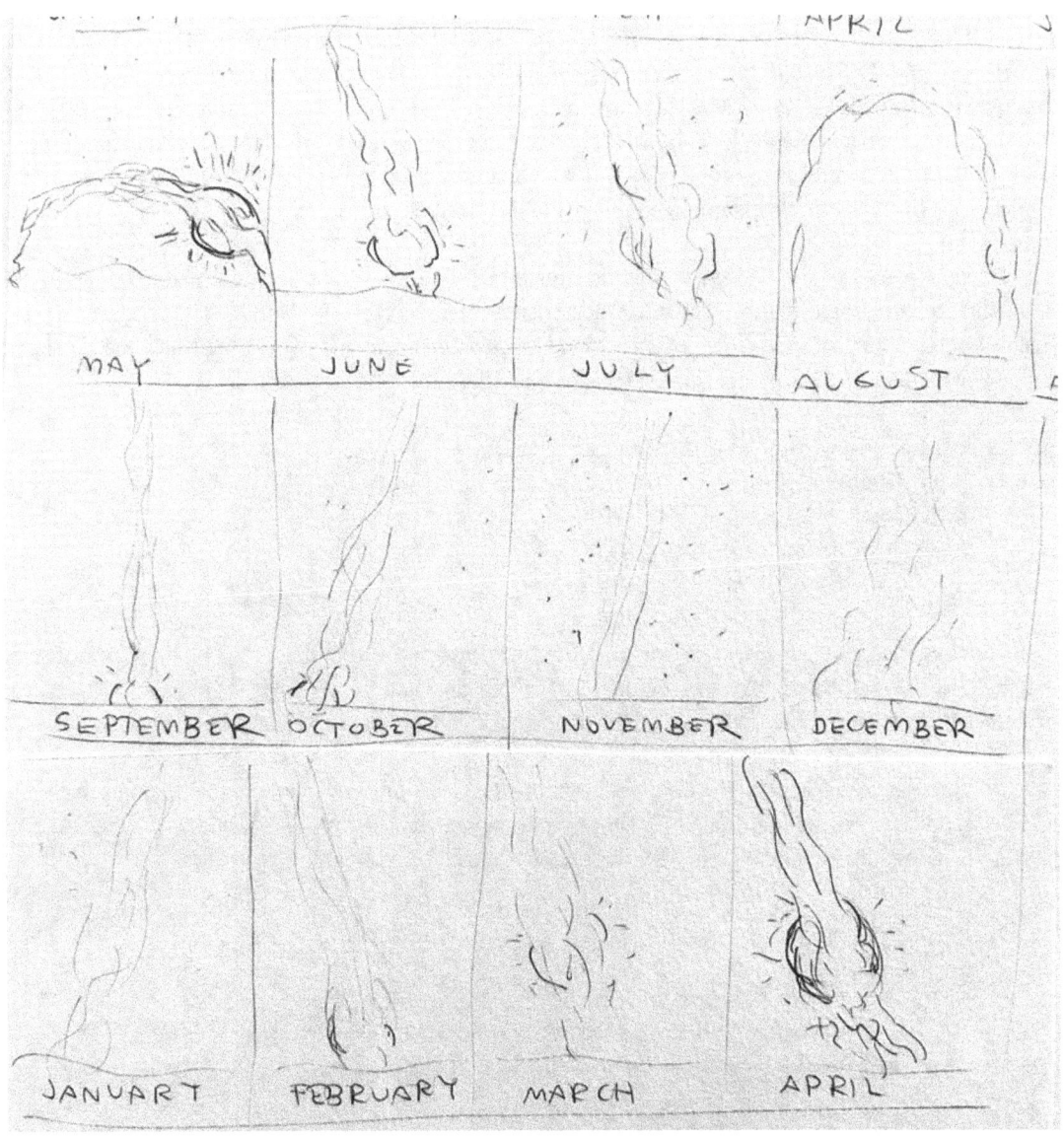

In the diagram above, here are 12 months of the Milky Way's Galactic Center, the envisioned pregnant belly of this Galaxy in the Southern Hemisphere's Divine Feminine half. As we see in the Somatic Rituals after it, May celebrates a culmination of the Galactic Center's Movements:

Starting in January, the Galactic Center (which contains the Gold and Silver gates that allow passage from Celelstial realms to earth) is not visible, and then it slowly becomes visible in the West, gradually moving East where it becomes prominent in May, in the brightest and longest view of the Galactic Center near the horizon at night. After May it begins to gradually not only appear moving west again, but it also begins to disappear for the winter months where it cannot be seen at all.* This information of the movements of the Galactic Center has been drawn by Karyn Crisis from the website of photographer Monika Deviat: monikadeviatphotography.com/12-months-of-milky-way/

===

Briefly, here is a last etymological journey to find the connections in this Strait to archaic history. First, recalling the: *"Egyptian belief that all celestial bodies rise, are born in the EAST and set, die down, in the WEST, so therefore the resurgent soul rose from the Southern Underworld in the EAST, Having previously (after death) entered that underworld in the WESTERN Mountain and Gate."* [204] And, that the purpose of entering the Underworld, for an advanced soul (there are many functions for different souls in the Underworld) is to move in a circular, clockwise motion beneath the earth's globe, into the Underworld (in Cosmic space) and then upwards to the Northern polar zone.

First note: *Chiesetta Madonna della Pieta* is situated on the Axis so that the door enters on the EAST and makes anyone entering (or the **Black Madonna** re-entering) face the WEST.
Second note: When entering *Chiesa Santa Margherita in Chianchetelle,* where the Madonna stays part of the year, one must enter on the West side to face the EAST.

pule = a gate, and is the same as pila, pillar, pilum shaft,
pulai = gates, **Mountain-passes, straits**;
pulis = small door
pulon = porch, gate, door
gate god **Pulas**, daugher was Pulia

Athene was called **Pulotis**, DeMeter was called also **Pulaia** and **Pulagora**, and **Pulos** the son of Ares and the Deity Thermo**Pulai**..all take their names from the gate, and **Pulai**Menes is one of the 12 zodiacal brothers who can only come into physical existence through another set of Gates.

So here, in this Mountain strait, are Pillars as the Gates of Heaven where the Madonna Ascends and Descends and people mimic this Motion by moving her icons from one locale to another. And in May, in fact, the Silver Gate of man is highlighted in Celestial movements.

===

MAY

As the Virgin Mary is referred to as the Happy Heavens Gates,
what does this have to do with Madonna icon Processions in the Month of May?

Earth is closest to the Milky Way Galactic Center in May and June, when Gemini and Taurus are activated as the Silver Gate of man, meaning "human." The Gates of Heaven are: Ursa Major and Ursa Minor, Arcturus protects them in the North. Arcturus' colors are ORANGE AND YELLOW, which are also said to be colors of the *femminielli who,* as part of tradition inherited from Corybantes, *would be protectors of the Triad Deity.* But, it's the Galactic Center gates that are celebrated in May as they

152

allow the **Black Madonna** to come down to earth, physically embodied once again (represented by her wooden statue or stone statues taken down from one locale to another and then back up again) before she returns to the Mountain via Ascension once again.

The Somatic Rituals listed below are celebrating the cycle of Ascent and Descent of the Polar Deity, here as the **Black Madonna** or other Madonnas. While this ritual is personified as a Deity coming down to earth (and reconnection via the Axis after the separation of the Heavens and Earth), it's also a Celestial event of the Milky Way as depicted in the chart above.

===

Somatic Rituals of Italy Celebrating the
Descent to earth of the Black Madonna
and her Ascent

- **Monte Viggiano** *La Madonna Nera del Sacro Monte di Viggiano*, Queen and Patroness of Lucania
  From May to September *La Madonna Nera* stays on the Mountain of *Sacro Monte*. The rest of the year La *Madonna Nera* stays down in the Basilica.

Myth: Boiled down to basics, this myth tells us: this **Black Madonna** was carved of wood and covered with gold around d 500 A.D., and housed in a Basilicata with a Roman name called Grumentum. During the Muslim invasion of the 8th and 9th centuries Grumentum was destroyed. Christian survivors took refuge in the mountains, taking the Madonna statue with them, wrapped in a mantle. They buried her in the earth up here, in a cave. In the 11th century sometimes, someone saw a blue flame on the mountain, followed it up the mountain and discovered the statue in the cave by digging it up. It was brought down to the village and a chapel was built by the cave, called *her place of hiding* and it's the sanctuary where she spends her summers.

Somatic ritual to remember:
1st Sunday May: Procession up to Mountain Sanctuary of the Sacred mountain
1st Sunday September: Descent to Basilica Santa Maria de Deposito
In May, the Galactic Center is also visible and has shifted from the West to the East
In September, the Galactic Center starts its descent below the horizon where it will disappear for the winter months completely.

===

This same Procession is done in **Vassviere**, France: where an icon spends its summers on a Mountain, and it is moved down in town for the fall season.

===

- **Chianchetelle**
The 1st Sunday of May, the wooden statue of the *Madonna della Pieta* is brought to the chapel *Chiesetta Madonna della Pieta* across from the Sabato river in the *stretto di Barba* for a celebration. This chapel is dedicated to her. In the afternoon, there is a traditional Procession where she is brought through the streets to Chianchetelle. Year-long she stays in a church in Chianchetelle, taken there via procession on foot. Then, the wooden statue is brought back May1st.

Keeping in mind that Water processions, where icons are taken: Out of a chapel, To the water, back to the chapel, into the waters and back demonstrates Ascension into IMMORTALITY in Polar Celetial space, through the Ursa Major and Minor Gates of Heaven.

Whereas in May and September, the Galactic Gates that allow Ascended Masters with a fixed Identity return to earth, if they choose, to inhabit that physial body they used to Indentify with as that Identity, before they then speed it up into light again and Ascend once more. Up and Down Mountain Rituals are demonstrating a temporary connection between the Heavens and Earth via the Milky Way as an Axis for the **Black Madonna** to return, in alignment with Divine Motion of the Milky Way movements of its Galactic Center going from North/West to South/East to the West/North once again, **Bringing heavens down to earth,** and then Ascending Divnity to the Polar North's Mountain Palace through the Ursa Gates.

> "Our Patroness,
> so beautiful with your crown
> and mantle filled with stars
> that are the most beautiful.
> Oh Madonna della Stella,
> **you are in the chapel**
> **where we celebrate in May**
> and join in a long pilgrimage,
> a pilgrimage of love
> which rejoices the heart.
> Oh band, music and orchestra,
> play for our Patroness.
> A choir dressed in white
> sings for our most shining star,
> our Madonna della Stella,
> the most beautiful one."[205]

This prayer, "The Patron of Craco" above, contains particular words of symbolic note:
- crown, represents the infinite circle of time as well as Immortal Polar Deities
- mantle filled with stars represents the Blue firmament and its stars
- the chapel represents the Celestial Heavens-Palace within the Black Stone Magnetic Mountain, part of an elaborate dwelling zone of Polar Deities
- where we celebrate in May represents Ascension to the Heavens-Palace, and the descent, or physical manifestation of a Polar Deity on earth, is reenacted through the somatic ritual of pilgrimage: taking a statue of a Madonna (or other Polar Deity) out of a chapel and into another one, or in a circular route returning, in end, where it began, at the start.
- pilgrimage is the Somatic act of the ritual
- choir dressed in white, singing songs encoded with Celestial knowledge, wearing white as the color of the Bright Heavens is one way secret spiritual groups practiced their orally contained memories and passed them down to others.

SUMMARY

The **Black Madonna**, or the older Deities they have replaced, represent specific places in the Cosmos, personified as a conscious Deities who are responsible for the Divine Motion of these Celestial places.

She may have many names attached to her core "Madonna" description, because this was done in archaic tradition: to give a Creator Deity a name, though it may present a star, a constellation, or an aspect of Divine Motion…and then give all of its Creations names that are based on its original name. Only much later in time did Deities begin having separate names that are disconnected from an etymology that reminds us of their connection to the Structure and Divine Motion of the Cosmos.

The **Black Madonnas** are envisioned as moving through the Heavens and Earth despite their separation long ago, using various Gates and Portals and in alignment with movements of the Milky Way and its Galactic Center which is attributed to the Divine Feminine.

Her other movements align with Celestial events in the sky: the Milky Way seems to turn horizontally and vertically depending on configurations of our planet's rotation, for example, and sometimes parts of the Milky Way seem to disappear depending on the hemisphere one is looking to the sky from. These movements are reflected not only in MYTHS of Deities disappearing or reappearing, but also in their accompanying Somatic Rituals, such as with the **Black Madonna** icons being taken Down from the mountain and then Back Up again, as Descending and Ascending, all in a larger celebration of the *Dancing of the Stars* in their circular or whirling movements.

WORDS WITH DOUBLE MEANINGS

- *Filastrocche* example:

"La Bella lavanderina" is a nursery rhyme, called *filastrocche* in Italian that
used to be commonly taught, but it contains hidden magical meanings.

For example, a washerwoman used to often also be the midwife (lavatrice and
levatrice) who knew magical rituals to help the mother-to-be during childbirth
and rituals to protect the newborn baby.

The jumping refers to jumping over the threshold, or "through the veil".

Pulling the tail of the cat refers to a magical rite done in energy battles: it's said that
if you see a Black cat near you, in your room perhaps, that's shadowy, you
should run to it and try to catch its tail because it's someone psychically
spying on you, and the act of catching its tail, if successful, can give you
an image of who the spy is.

Turning around refers to making a circle towards the 4 Cardinal Direction,
which is also a protective measure.

Rolling eyes up and down is honoring the Celestial space as well as earth.

Giving a kiss means to initiate someone, who will then in turn initiate the
next person within the sacred circle.

===

"La Bella lavanderina"

The beautiful washerwoman
who washes diapers; jump in, make another one,
pull the tail of the cat,
pull the bells, turn around, do it again,
roll your eyes, lower your eyes down: give a kiss to whoever you want
…
La bella lavanderina
che lava i pannolini;
fai un salto, fanne un altro,
tira la coda al gatto, tira le campanelle, fai una giravolta, fallo un'altra volta, alza gli occhi al cielo,
abbassa gli occhi in giù:
dai un bacio a chi vuoi tu.

This prayer to Santa Lucia speaks to the spirit of fennel, asks for a circle of protection, and asks
Santa Lucia to go to her house (in Celestial space) to get fennel, the spirit-form.

"Santa Lucia
entra a casa mia
co' 'n mazzo de finocchio.

Santa Lucia, santa Lucia,
passa 'ntorno a casa mia,
co' 'n mazzu de finocchiu
puliscime bene l'occhiu

Santa Lucia, va' la a casa tua
prendi 'n po' de finocchi
e puliscime quest'occhi"

"Saint Lucia
enter my house
with a bunch of fennel.

 Saint Lucia, Saint Lucia,
pass around my house,
with a bunch of fennel
clean my eye well

Santa Lucia, go to your house
take some fennel
and clean these eyes"

From Mario Polia "Tra Cielo e terra: Cosi pregavano I nostri padri", (Editrice Centro Italia, 2009)

1. Dr John Knight Lundwall, "The Mythic Canon: How Oral Poeple Transmit Sacred Knowledge", https://www.youtube.com/watch?v=QLR5cemNV7E

2. John O'Neill, "The Night of the Gods An Inquiry into Cosmic and Cosmogonic Mythology and Symbolism,Vol II." , (David Nutt 270 & 271 Strand, 1897), London, p. 935

3. MythVision Podcast (TheWaterBoyZ) "Mythos & Cosmos: Mind and Meaning in the Oral Age with John K Lundwall (TheWaterBoyz), Oct 26, 2018, Youtube interview, (37:08-39:56)

4. ibid.

5. *phrase coined by Dr John Knight Lundwall in audio interviews

6. John O'Neill, "The Night of the Gods, An Inquiry into Cosmic and Cosmogonic Mythology and Symbolism Vol I", (Bernard Quaritch, 1893) London, p.118

7. Lundwall, Dr J.K., "The Mythic Canon: How Oral Poeple Transmit Sacred Knowledge" Youtube, April 24, 2020, https://www.youtube.com/watch?v=QLR5cemNV7E

8. ibid.

9. O'Neill, J. "The Night of the Gods, Vol I", (Bernard Quaritch, 1893) London, p.126

10. ibid., p.131 Arabic treatise on stones

11. O'Neill, J. "The Night of the Gods,Vol II.", (David Nutt 270 & 271 Strand, 1897), London, p.804

12. O'Neill, J. "The Night of the Gods, Vol I", (Bernard Quaritch, 1893) London, p.291

13. ibid, (297,298)

14. O'Neill, J. "The Night of the Gods,Vol II.", (David Nutt 270 & 271 Strand, 1897), London, p.1033

15 ibid.

16 ibid.

17 ibid.

18. Friedrich Wilhelm Bergmann, "La fascination de Gulfi (Gylfa Ginning)", (Strasbourg, Treuttel, 1871), p.262

19. O'Neill, J. "The Night of the Gods, Vol I ", (Bernard Quaritch, 1893) London, p. 156

20. ibid., p.142

21. ibid., p.143

22. ibid., p.144

23 Lundwall, Dr J.K., various audio iterviews

24. Marija Gimbutas, "The Language of the Goddess" (Harper & Row, 1989). p. 200

25. O'Neill, J. "The Night of the Gods, Vol I ", (Bernard Quaritch, 1893) London, p.112

26. ibid., p.122

27. ibid., p.126

28. ibid., p.122

29. ibid., p.127

30. ibid.

31. ibid., p.107

32. ibid., p.113

33. ibid., p.115

34. ibid.

35. ibid., p.203

36. ibid.

37. ibid., p.117

38. ibid., p.223, 273

39. ibid., p.121

40. ibid.

41. ibid., p.95

42. MythVision Podcast "Jesus & Orion Astrotheology with John K Lundwall" (part 5 of 6), May 15, 2019, Youtube interview, (54:26-56:30)

43. O'Neill, J. "The Night of the Gods, Vol I" , (Bernard Quaritch, 1893) London, p.129

44. ibid., p.131

45. O'Neill, J. "The Night of the Gods, Vol II.", (David Nutt 270 & 271 Strand, 1897), London, p.926

46. O'Neill, J. "The Night of the Gods, Vol I", (Bernard Quaritch, 1893) London, p.94

47. ibid., p.115

48. ibid., p.385

49. https://www.interfaithmary.net/Black-madonna-index/costa-rica

50. https://www.interfaithmary.net/Black-madonna-index/oirschot

51. O'Neill, J. "The Night of the Gods, Vol I", (Bernard Quaritch, 1893) London, p. 94

52. ibid., p.142

53.   ibid., p.104:

54.   Mario Polia, "Tra Cielo e terra: Cosi pregavano I nostri padri: Preghiere popolari delle Valentina" (Editrice Centro Italia, 2009) , p.845

55.   O'Neill, J. "The Night of the Gods, Vol I", (Bernard Quaritch, 1893) London, p.520

56.   ibid., p.486

57.   Polia, M. Mario"Tra Cielo e terra: Cosi pregavano I nostri padri", (Editrice Centro Italia, 2009), p.845

58.   Kile Smith, "Ave Maris Stella", KileSmith.com, Sep 3, 2021,   https://kilesmith.com/2021/09/03/ave-maris-stella/

59.   Valentinas Mite, "Iraq: Old Sabaean-Mandean Community Is Proud of Its Ancient Faith", Radio Free Europe, July 14, 2004, https://www.rferl.org/a/1053864.html

60.   O'Neill, J. "The Night of the Gods, Vol I", (Bernard Quaritch, 1893) London, p.507

61.   ibid., p.508

62.   ibid., p.106

63.   ibid., p.129

64.   ibid., p.507

65.   ibid., p.37

66.   https://it.wikipedia.org/wiki/Varia_di_Palmi

67.   O'Neill, J. "The Night of the Gods,Vol II.", (David Nutt 270 & 271 Strand, 1897), London, p.723

68   ibid.

69.   Lundwall, J.K. MythVision Podcast "Jesus & Orion Astrotheology with John K Lundwall" (part 5 of 6), May 15, 2019,Youtube interview, (54:26-56:30)

70.   O'Neill, J. "The Night of the Gods, Vol I", (Bernard Quaritch, 1893) London, p.122

71.   ibid., p.307

72.   ibid., p.71

73.   William F. Warren, S.T.D.,LL.D., "Paradise Found, The cradle of the Human Race at the North Pole, A Study of the Prehistoric World," (Houghton, Mifflin and Company, Boston, 1885, 6th Edition), p.250

74.   ibid., p.253

75.   O'Neill, J. "The Night of the Gods,Vol II.", (David Nutt 270 & 271 Strand, 1897), London, p.723

76.   ibid., p.832

77.   O'Neill, J. "The Night of the Gods, Vol I", (Bernard Quaritch, 1893) London, p.315

78.   ibid., p.320

79.   ibid., p.316

80.   O'Neill, J. "The Night of the Gods, Vol II.", (David Nutt 270 & 271 Strand, 1897), London, p.832

81.   ibid.

82.   ibid., p.121

83.   O'Neill, J. "The Night of the Gods, Vol II.", (David Nutt 270 & 271 Strand, 1897), London, p.952

82.   Lundwall, J. "The Mythic Canon: How Oral Poeple Transmit Sacred Knowledge", https://www.youtube.com/watch?v=QLR5cemNV7E

83.   image from: https://www.biblicalarchaeology.org/daily/biblical-sites-places/biblical-archaeology-sites/earliest-image-of-the-virgin-mary-dura-europos-church/

84.   John Lundwall

85.   ibid

86.   O'Neill, J. "The Night of the Gods, Vol I", (Bernard Quaritch, 1893) London, p.110

87.   https://www.midi-france.info/030701a_st_sara.htm

88.   O'Neill, J. "The Night of the Gods, Vol I", (Bernard Quaritch, 1893) London, p.51

89.   O'Neill, J. "The Night of the Gods, Vol II.", (David Nutt 270 & 271 Strand, 1897), London, p.1034

90.   ibid.

91.   O'Neill, J. "The Night of the Gods, Vol II.", (David Nutt 270 & 271 Strand, 1897), London, p.901

92.   ibid.,p.715

93.   ibid., p.1031

94.   ibid.

95.   ibid.

96.   ibid.

97.   Austen Henry Layard, "Nineveh and Babylon", (London John Murray, 1882), p.367

98.   ibid., p.851

99.   ibid., p.717

100.   O'Neill, J. "The Night of the Gods, Vol II.", (David Nutt 270 & 271 Strand, 1897), p.861

101. ibid., p.867

102. ibid., p.721

103. ibid., p. 228

104. O'Neill, J. "The Night of the Gods,Vol II.", (David Nutt 270 & 271 Strand, 1897), p.682.

105 Polia, M. Mario"Tra Cielo e terra: Cosi pregavano I nostri padri", (Editrice Centro Italia, 2009), p.273, 274

106. ibid., p.292

107 ibid.

108. ibid., p.181

109. ibid., p.306

110. ibid., p.355

111. ibid., p.343

112. ibid., p.153

113. ibid.

114. ibid.

114. ibid., p.306,307

115. ibid., p.119

116. Rig Vevda, iii,49

117. O'Neill, J. "The Night of the Gods,Vol II.", (David Nutt 270 & 271 Strand, 1897), p.884

118. O'Neill, J. "The Night of the Gods, Vol I", (Bernard Quaritch, 1893), p.506

119. Prof. John Perry, "Romance of Science: Spinning Tops". (E&JB Young & Co,1890) p107-110.

120. O'Neill, J. "The Night of the Gods, Vol I", (Bernard Quaritch, 1893), p.306

121. O'Neill, J. "The Night of the Gods,Vol II.", (David Nutt 270 & 271 Strand, 1897), p.628

122. ibid., p.1389

122. O'Neill, J. "The Night of the Gods, Vol I", (Bernard Quaritch, 1893), p.389

124. Francois Lenormant, "Les origines de l'histoire d'apres la Bible e les traditions de peuples orientaux", (Maisonneuve, 1880), p.300

125. O'Neill, J. "The Night of the Gods, Vol I", (Bernard Quaritch, 1893), p.300

126. ibid., p.300

127. ibid., p.744

128. ibid., p.344

129. ibid., p.347

130. ibid., p.427

131. Polia, M. "Tra Cielo e terra: Cosi pregavano I nostri padri: Preghiere popolari delle Valentina" (Editrice Centro Italia, 2009)

132. O'Neill, J. "The Night of the Gods, Vol I", (Bernard Quaritch, 1893), p.196

133. ibid., p.381

134. W.R.S. Ralston, M.A., "Russian Folk Tales", (R. Worthington, 750 Broadway, NY 1880), p.134

135. Ivar Nielsen, Native-Science.net, https://www.native-science.net/Milky_Way_Myths.htm

136. O'Neill, J. "The Night of the Gods, Vol II.", (David Nutt 270 & 271 Strand, 1897), p.898

137. O'Neill, J. "The Night of the Gods, Vol I", (Bernard Quaritch, 1893), p.194

138. ibid., p.195

139. ibid., p.95

140. ibid

141. O'Neill, J. "The Night of the Gods, Vol II.", (David Nutt 270 & 271 Strand, 1897), p.682

142. https://handmaidsoftheimmaculate.weebly.com/blog/the-story-of-our-lady-of-the-pillar

143. http://forosdelavirgen.org/342/virgen-del-pilar-espana-12-de-octubre/

144. Andiamocene alla montagne source https://www.facebook.com/people/Fuochi-nella-nebbia, February 2, 2020

145. O'Neill, J. "The Night of the Gods, Vol II.", (David Nutt 270 & 271 Strand, 1897), p.692

146. ibid., p.913

147. O'Neill, J. "The Night of the Gods, Vol I", (Bernard Quaritch, 1893), p.370

148. ibid.

149. ibid., p.122

150. ibid

151. ibid

152. O'Neill, J. "The Night of the Gods, Vol II.", (David Nutt 270 & 271 Strand, 1897), p.678

153. ibid., p.686

154. ibid., p.913

155. ibid., p.704

156. O'Neill, J. "The Night of the Gods, Vol I", (Bernard Quaritch, 1893), p.289

157. O'Neill, J. "The Night of the Gods, Vol II.", (David Nutt 270 & 271 Strand, 1897), p.1221

158. O'Neill, J. "The Night of the Gods, Vol I", (Bernard Quaritch, 1893), p.121

159. Apollonius Rhodius, Argonautica 2, https://www.theoi.com/Olympios/AresFavour.html

160. O'Neill, J. "The Night of the Gods, Vol II.", (David Nutt 270 & 271 Strand, 1897), p.686

161. O'Neill, J. "The Night of the Gods, Vol I", (Bernard Quaritch, 1893), p.94

162. ibid., p.194

163. ibid., p.384

164. ibid., p.529

165. Irving Goldman, "The Mouth of Heaven: An Introduction to Kwakiutl Religious Thought" (Wiley,1975) p.195

166. O'Neill, J. "The Night of the Gods, Vol I", (Bernard Quaritch, 1893), p.227

167. ibid., p.368

168. ibid., p.307

169. ibid., p.367

170. ibid., p.368

171. ibid., p.307

172. ibid., p.385

173. O'Neill, J. "The Night of the Gods, Vol II.", (David Nutt 270 & 271 Strand, 1897), p.914

174. Lundwall, J.K. MythVision Podcast "Jesus & Orion Astrotheology with John K Lundwall" (part 5 of 6) ,May 15, 2019,Youtube interview, (24:07-24:58)

175. Marina Terragni, "Trans, "femminielli" and the mother's body", Sept 1, 2021, https://feministpost.it/magazine/english/trans-femminielli-and-the-mothers-body/176. Varro, Lingua Latina. vi, t6 Seal0

177. Varro, Linngua Latina vii, 3, 86

178. O'Neill, J. "The Night of the Gods, Vol II.", (David Nutt 270 & 271 Strand, 1897), p.841

179. ibid., p.718

180. ibid., p/568

181. MythVision Podcast (TheWaterBoyZ) "Mythos & Cosmos: Mind and Meaning in the Oral Age with John K Lundwall (TheWaterBoyz), Oct 26, 2018, Youtube interview, 36:37

182. MythVision Podcast (TheWaterBoyZ) "Mythos & Cosmos: Mind and Meaning in the Oral Age with John K Lundwall (TheWaterBoyz), Oct 26, 2018, Youtube interview, (31:56)

183. Neilsen, I., Native-Science.net, https://www.native-science.net/Milky_Way_Myths.htm (Curtis 1921; 82)

184. O'Neill, J. "The Night of the Gods, Vol I", (Bernard Quaritch, 1893), p.37

185. Andrew Lang, M.A., "Custom and Myth", (Longmans, Green, And Co, London, 1884) p.48

REFERENCE NOTES

186. O'Neill, J. "The Night of the Gods, Vol I", (Bernard Quaritch, 1893), p. 297

187. Lewis and Clarke, "Expedition", (Philadelphia, 1814), p. 139 (in Tylor)

188. George Turner, "Samoa a Hundred Years ago", (American Association for the Advancement of Science, 1884), p.198

189. O'Neill, J. "The Night of the Gods, Vol I", (Bernard Quaritch, 1893), p.8

190. ibid., p.38

191. O'Neill, J. "The Night of the Gods, Vol II.", (David Nutt 270 & 271 Strand, 1897), p.686

192. ibid., p.515

193. https://www.cumpagniadiventemigliusi.it/vecchiosito/Tradizioni_Intemelie/Barca-testo-spartito.htm

194. https://www.rivieratime.news/bajardo-la-festa-della-ra-barca-una-tradizione-antica-di-800-anni/

195. MythVision Podcast "Jesus & Orion Astrotheology with John K Lundwall" (part 6 of 6), May 15, 2019, Youtube interview, (4:36)

196. O'Neill, J. "The Night of the Gods, Vol II.", (David Nutt 270 & 271 Strand, 1897), p.1007

197. O'Neill, J. "The Night of the Gods, Vol I", (Bernard Quaritch, 1893), p.148

198. ibid., p.305

199. ibid., p.176

200. ibid.

201. ibid., p.117

202. ibid., p.37,

203. Carlo Napolitano, "Il guardiano di Pietra. Sulle tracce del sabba e della grande madre nel Sannio Campano", (CSA Editrice, January 1, 2015)

204. O'Neill, J. "The Night of the Gods, Vol I", (Bernard Quaritch, 1893), p.251

205. The Patron of Craco reprinted from Homage to the Madonna della Stella, a publication of the Colibri Association and translated by the Craco Society, 2010, p.40

www.ingramcontent.com/pod-product-compliance
Lightning Source LLC
Chambersburg PA
CBHW081534120626

46550CB00009B/2724